THE THEATRE AND HISPANIC LIFE

Essays in Honour of
NEALE H. TAYLER

Edited by
A. A. Borrás

This collection of essays relates Spanish drama to Hispanic life from the late Middle Ages to the present. The volume opens with "Spanish Drama and its Foreign Affiliates," a discussion by W. T. McCready of the many interactions between Spanish and English, French, and German drama. J. H. Parker follows with a discussion of the modernity of Lope de Vega's plays, a modernity of theme and psychology. T. B. Barclay's "Reflections of Reality" provides intriguing comment upon Spanish drama in the eighteenth century, when it followed a French artistic formula, and in the Romantic period, during which purity of form was abandoned. Borrás's "Twentieth-Century Spanish Drama: In Defense of Liberty" thoughtfully examines the attack of modern theatre, including exiled playwrights, upon traditional, narrow, intolerant Spain. The final essay, Levy's "Ideology and Stagecraft in the Hispanic American Theatre of the 1960s," is a comprehensive review of the social commitment of the theatre of this period, a theatre which strove, above all, to shock the bourgeois out of complacency.

Spanish drama has been a special interest of Neale H. Tayler, the honoree; the volume marks his retirement as President of Wilfrid Laurier University.

A. A. Borrás, who received the Ph.D. from The Pennsylvania State University, specializes in contemporary Spanish literature. He currently teaches in, and is chairman of, the Department of Romance Languages at Wilfrid Laurier University. He is the author of El teatro del exilio de Max Aub. *The other contributors all teach at the University of Toronto.*

THE
THEATRE
AND
HISPANIC LIFE

Essays in Honour of
NEALE H. TAYLER

THE
THEATRE
AND
HISPANIC LIFE

Essays in Honour of
NEALE H. TAYLER

Edited by
A. A. Borrás

Wilfrid Laurier University Press

Canadian Cataloguing in Publication Data

Main entry under title:
The Theatre and Hispanic life : essays in honour of
Neale H. Tayler

ISBN 0-88920-129-3

1. Spanish drama − History and criticism − Addresses,
essays, lectures. 2. Theater − Spain − History −
Addresses, essays, lectures. 3. Tayler, Neale H.
(Neale Hamilton), 1917-   I. Tayler, Neale H.
(Neale Hamilton), 1917-   II. Borrás, A. A. (Angelo
Augusto), 1935-

PQ6099.T48   862'.009   C82-094726-1

Copyright © 1982

WILFRID LAURIER UNIVERSITY PRESS
Waterloo, Ontario, Canada   N2L 3C5

82 83 84 85 4 3 2 1

CONTENTS

NOTES ON CONTRIBUTORS

Warren T. McCready, Ph.D., professor of Spanish and Portuguese at the University of Toronto, is a specialist in Spanish Drama and Bibliography. He is the author of *Bibliografía temática de estudios sobre el teatro español antiguo* and of other critical works in his field.

J. H. Parker, Ph.D., F.R.S.C., professor at the University of Toronto, is a specialist in sixteenth- and seventeenth-century Spanish and Portuguese literatures. He is the author of *Gil Vicente*, *Juan Pérez de Montalván*, and of other books on Golden Age literature.

T. B. Barclay, Ph.D., teaches Spanish and Portuguese at the University of Toronto. He is a specialist in Spanish contemporary theatre.

A. A. Borrás, Ph.D., is professor of Spanish and chairman of the Department of Romance Languages at Wilfrid Laurier University. He is the author of *El teatro del exilio de Max Aub*, and has written many articles on Spanish contemporary literature, his area of specialization.

Kurt L. Levy, Ph.D., F.R.S.C., professor and chairman of the Department of Spanish and Portuguese at the University of Toronto, specializes in Spanish-American Literature. He is the author of three major volumes on Tomás Carrasquilla and other critical works in his field.

FOREWORD

D **r. Neale H. Tayler,** President of Wilfrid Laurier University, was born in Windsor, Ontario, June 16, 1917. He received his B.A., M.A., and Ph.D. degrees from the University of Toronto. His doctoral studies were in Romance Languages; his area of specialization, nineteenth-century Spanish theatre, specifically that of Manuel Tamayo y Baus. It is fitting, then, that this volume, prepared in his honour, treats the theme of Spanish Theatre and Hispanic Life. Indeed, his favourite genre, the one to which his interests have been oriented throughout his career, is the drama.

Apart from the year 1946-47, when Dr. Tayler taught at the University of Western Ontario, he spent the early part of his career, between 1941 and 1962, teaching at the University of Toronto, his *alma mater*. In 1962 he joined Waterloo Lutheran University, which became Wilfrid Laurier University in November 1973. During the period 1962-68, he served as Chairman of the Department of Romance Languages at W.L.U. and was instrumental in establishing graduate programmes in Spanish and French. In 1968 he became Dean of the Faculty of Arts and Science, and in 1972 Vice President:

Academic. Six years later, in 1978, he became the second president of Wilfrid Laurier University.

When Dr. Tayler became President in 1978, I succeeded him as Vice President: Academic, and, in that capacity, I have worked closely with him for the past four years. During that period, I came to know him well and learned to rely on his excellent judgment and sense of timing. While his manner was quiet and tactful, his resolve was always firm. He knew where he wanted the institution to go, and he led it there. He has earned the admiration and gratitude of the entire Wilfrid Laurier University community.

John A. Weir
Vice President: Academic

INTRODUCTION

"The Theatre and Hispanic Life," the title for the collection of essays which comprise the *Festschrift*, might also be considered an appropriate identification of Professor Tayler's areas of interest and expertise. As a professor of Spanish Language and Literature, he has shared his knowledge and appreciation of Hispanic culture with students and colleagues alike over the years. His co-authored books, *La vida española* and *Lecturas iberoamericanas*, have served as an engaging introduction to Spanish literature and civilization. In the area of the theatre, he has made a valuable contribution to Spanish scholarship with his book, *Las fuentes del teatro de Tamayo y Baus*.

The five essays contained herein relate the theatre to Hispanic life from the late Middle Ages to present times. Each epoch shows social, political, philosophical, and esthetic differences, but what remains constant in Spanish literature is the portrayal of the individual member of society, man himself, his soul laid bare before the harsh realities about him.

Warren T. McCready's essay, "Spanish Drama and its Foreign Affiliates," serves well to show how the literatures of Europe are interrelated in themes, partly because of the rediscovery of the classics in the Renaissance period, a period in which translations and adaptations of Greek and Roman drama were abundant. McCready observes that Spanish literature had a real impact on European drama, as the personalities of Don Juan, Don Quixote, and Don Carlos attest. The "humanistic" element of drama is highlighted throughout the essay, so that all the borrowings, translations, adaptations, and simultaneous expressions come to be understood as mere reflections of common curiosities shared by all humanity.

In his essay, "Lope de Vega: Eternally Popular and Modern," Jack H. Parker asserts that the theatrically educated public, capable of understanding, admiring, and following all types of Golden Age dramas, certainly did influence the content and course of Lopean drama. Cloak and sword plays, although entertaining and popular, nevertheless dealt with universal emotions and interests. Their prevailing psychology is as relevant today. Observing that the Golden Age drama reflects the society of the time, Parker finds the drama's influence on society more difficult to assess. He concludes that it was up to the people to reject or accept the lessons to be learned; certainly Lope de Vega was no moralist, but some of his contemporaries were.

While Spanish theatre in almost every epoch reflects the respective manners, speech, fads, customs, and cultural trivia, there are two short-lived exceptions. T. B. Barclay, in his "Reflections of Reality," comments on these two periods. In the eighteenth century the fashionable writer followed a French artistic formula, and during the Romantic period (between 1833 and 1850, approximately) purity of form was abandoned in order to achieve a spirit of freedom and individualism. It is Ramón de la Cruz's delightful playlets, however, whose amusing scenes of striking realism captured life as it was at the moment. Barclay's carefully selected examples of manifestations of the times with regard to dress, music, instruments, dance forms, and customs provide a vivid picture of nineteenth-century Spain. Less positive views are expressed by other dramatists, however, such as Moratín and

Jovellanos. The century is well advanced before dramatists turn their attention to the society of their time; it is Tamayo y Baus who sees an ethical crisis in the nation which must be combatted with Christian love and charity.

Jacinto Benavente delighted audiences with his psychological and satirical plays in which his scepticism and mistrust for society is countered by his belief in love as an ennobling sentiment. In his essay, "Twentieth-Century Spanish Drama: In Defense of Liberty," A. A. Borrás follows the trajectory of twentieth-century Spanish theatre, of which Benavente is considered the father. García Lorca and Valle-Inclán created innovations in the theatre, each drawing inspiration from the folklore of his native region. Their plays reveal an attack on traditional, narrow, intolerant Spain. Valle-Inclán's increasingly negative view of the world reaches its peak in his *esperpentos* wherein Spain is seen as a grotesque deformation of European civilization. The Spanish Civil War created an exile theatre whose artistic expression of conditions of isolation and alienation from the homeland is of superior quality. The post-war, government-imposed censorship did not totally succeed in stifling the production of a social theatre. Buero Vallejo, one of Spain's foremost dramatists, for example, has had substantial success in launching a theatre of social protest in which the poor and humble of society are seen to live a life of frustration and despair but not necessarily defeat. Contemporary Spanish theatre, by the indication of such authors as Carlos Muñiz and Lauro Olmo, will continue the process of constant revitalization and the tradition of protesting oppressive social conditions.

Kurt L. Levy's essay, "Ideology and Stagecraft in the Hispanic American Theatre of the 1960s," makes a strong comprehensive statement on the social commitment of the theatre of this period, a theatre "of living people, close to Latin America's social reality and its individual and collective hopes and fears." Levy chooses six representative dramatists who show varying techniques of shocking the bourgeois out of complacency. Ideological debates such as those between the powerful industrialist and his conscience in Egon Wolff's *Los invasores* abound; the challenge of giving

voice to the American conscience, the native essence of which
is the cultural legacy of the protagonists in René Marqués' *El
apartamiento*, is presented. Collective guilt is the theme of
another drama, Carlos Gorostiza's *El pan de la locura*,
wherein the universal problem of fear and cowardice, the
inhibitors of responsibility, is evident. Doubtless, for all six
authors, theatre must be instrumental in bringing about
social change.

It is hoped that the many friends and colleagues of Dr.
Neale H. Tayler will find something of interest and enjoy-
ment in this collection of essays entitled *The Theatre and
Hispanic Life*. To the neophyte and to the seasoned student of
Spanish drama as well, it is the authors' wish that this volume
will serve a didactic purpose. And for the retiring President
of Wilfrid Laurier University, we trust that this homage will
be a living memento of his accomplishments of the past and a
salutation for a future of continued success and fulfillment.

Waterloo, Ontario   *A. A. Borrás*
September 1981

ONE

SPANISH DRAMA AND ITS FOREIGN AFFILIATES

Warren T. McCready
University of Toronto

During the Renaissance, European nations, including Spain, rediscovered the classics; translations and adaptations of Greek and Roman drama, among other writings, were made in abundance. In Spain, Francisco López de Villalobos made the first translation into Spanish of Plautus' *Amphitruo* (1515). From his free prose translation Juan Timoneda (d. 1583) made an acting version, *Amphitrión*. This play and his *Los Menemnos*, or *Menecmos*, a translation or close adaptation of *Menaechmi*, "were the first appearance of Plautus on the Spanish stage."[1] Incidentally, did Jean Giraudoux know of Timoneda? If not, his *Amphitryon 38* ought to be *Amphitryon 39*. Molière also wrote an

---

1 J. P. W. Crawford, *Spanish Drama Before Lope de Vega* (Philadelphia: University of Pennsylvania Press, 1967), 124.

Amphitrion. Later in the century Juan de la Cueva (1550?-1610?) wrote his *Tragedia de la muerte de Virginia y Appio Claudio*, performed in Seville in 1580. In the eighteenth century the Italian Vittorio Alfieri wrote his *Virginia*, and in 1853 it was done again in Spain by Manuel Tamayo y Baus (1829-1898) (M1496).[2] (On the work of this dramatist a book has been written by our ex-colleague and president *jubilante* of Wilfrid Laurier University, Neale Tayler.) Many more works based on the classics were written in European languages, but let these suffice for our purpose.

As Italy was the first beneficiary of the Renaissance, so its literature in turn became the source of inspiration for writers of other nations. In the prologue to his *Amphitrión* Timoneda presents a question of love in a dialogue in which two shepherds declare their love for a girl and want to know which one she prefers. She answers by giving a garland to one and accepting a wreath from the other. The source of this question is the fourth part of Boccaccio's *Filocolo*, in which Fiammetta proposes a series of thirteen "questioni d'amore." It is the first of the thirteen. This question was used by Cervantes in the third act of his play *La entretenida*, and it is also found in a play attributed to Lope de Vega (1562-1635), *El premio riguroso y amistad bien pagada* (*The Rigorous Prize and Friendship Well Paid*) (M26, 559). Such borrowings of "bits and pieces" by one author or literature from another are abundant in all ages; this example serves merely as a starting point.

Boccaccio's *Decameron* (Day VII, tale 9) is the source of the ancient Spanish *Entremés de un viejo que es casado con una mujer moza* (*Interlude of an Old Man Married to a Young Woman*), and the same story is found in *El viejo celoso* (*The Jealous Old Man*), one of Cervantes' eight *entremeses* (M11).

---

2 General information may be found in histories of literature, but more detailed references are in my *Bibliografía temática de estudios sobre el teatro español antiguo* (Toronto: University of Toronto Press, 1966) and in Hilda U. Stubbings, *Renaissance Spain in its Literary Relations with England and France: A Critical Bibliography* (Nashville: Vanderbilt University Press, 1968). To avoid a superfluity of footnotes, these works are indicated in the text by M or S followed by the item number.

Lope de Vega, Spain's greatest dramatist, wrote *El ejemplo de casadas y prueba de la paciencia* (*The Paragon of Wives and Test of Patience*) at about the end of the sixteenth century. His source was the last tale of the *Decameron* (x, 10), the widely known story of the "patient Griselda." Earlier, Timoneda had told the same story in the second "patraña" of his *Patrañuelo*, a collection of twenty-two tales, or short stories, taken from various sources. Still earlier it had been the subject of the "Clerk's Tale" in Chaucer's *Canterbury Tales*. Again in England, at about the same time as Lope de Vega's play, Thomas Dekker in collaboration with Henry Chettle and William Haughton wrote the comedy called *Patient Grissil* (1598). In 1835 Friedrich Halm (pseudonym of Baron Eligius Franz Joseph von Münch-Bellinghausen, the Austrian dramatist) wrote his play *Griseldis* in which the heroine for the first time spoke up on behalf of the wife's role in marriage. In this century the German playwright Gerhart Hauptmann added his *Griselda* (1909) to the other versions. Also from Boccaccio's *Decameron* (ii, 9) comes the tale of the scoundrel who, unable to seduce the faithful wife of an acquaintance, bribes a servant to give him intimate details of the lady, such as only a lover would be apt to know—a mole on her back or thigh, the way to and from her bedroom, etc. He then claims that he has slept with her and offers these facts as proof. This is the plot of *Eufemia*, a play by the Spanish dramatist Lope de Rueda (1510?-1565). Since Juan Timoneda was the publisher of Rueda's works, it is not surprising that the story appears in Patraña 15 of his *Patrañuelo* (1567), and forty-odd years later it turns up as Shakespeare's *Cymbeline*. It should be understood that none of the analogues presented here are direct copies or translations. Each work is changed to some extent as it passes through translations from one language, time, country, and author to another.

Juan de la Cueva, the principal predecessor of Lope de Vega, wrote a play called *El degollado* (*The Decapitated One*), based on a tale in the *Hecatommiti* (Decade viii, tale 5) by Giovan Battista Giraldi Cintio. A Spanish lady and her lover are captured by Moorish soldiers and taken to their prince.

The prince threatens to have the lover beheaded unless the
lady submits herself to him. The same plot is found, but in
different circumstances, in Shakespeare's *Measure for Measure* (M96, S192).

Another Italian writer whose works were widely read, translated, and imitated was Matteo Bandello (1485-1562). From
Part II, tale 9 of his *Novelle* comes Shakespeare's universally
known *Romeo and Juliet* and the not so well known
play by Lope de Vega, *Castelvines y Monteses* (the names
corresponding to Capulets and Montagues). The greatest
difference between the two plays is that in the Spanish (written about 1606-1612) the lovers survive; consequently it has a
happy ending (M3620, S356). Much earlier, possibly as early
as 1537 or 1538, Lope de Rueda wrote a play called *Los
engañados*, adapted from the Italian play *Gl'Ingannati (The
Deceived)*, written by members of the Accademia degli Intro-
nati. The plot is found in Bandello (I, 36), but it has echoes of
Plautus in that it treats of the confusion caused by the identical appearance of twins. In Rueda's play Fabricio and Lelia
are twin brother and sister. The boy was lost at the age of six
in Rome; Lelia grows up in a convent in Modena, but escapes
occasionally and falls in love with Lauro. Gerardo, a widower
and father of Clavela, wishes to marry Lelia. Lauro, because
of long absences from Lelia, is attracted to Clavela. Lelia, in
order to get Lauro back, disguises herself as a page and is
hired by him unknowingly. Clavela, wooed by Lauro, is
smitten with his "page," Fabio, but this is an impossible
combination. The whole situation is finally clarified when
the lost Fabricio arrives, is mistaken for "Fabio," whose true
identity is then revealed, and the lovers are paired off—
Lauro and Lelia, Fabricio and Clavela. This story forms the
plot of Shakespeare's *Twelfth Night*. In a simplified form it
appeared as the story of Felix and Felismena in the Spanish
pastoral novel *Diana* (circa 1559), by Jorge de Montemayor;
this in turn led to Shakespeare's play *Two Gentlemen of Verona*
(M540, S59).

The Catalan romance of chivalry, *Tirant lo Blanc*, by
Joanot Martorell, was published in Valencia in 1490. A
Spanish translation appeared in 1511. One of the episodes

concerns the frustrated love of the "Viuda reposada" (the solemn widow) for the hero, Tirant, who is to marry the princess Carmesina. The widow has a servant dress up as one of Tirant's rivals for the hand of the princess and, with Tirant as a witness, stages a false love scene with the princess. Eventually the ruse is discovered and the perpetrators are punished. This story was used by Ariosto in Canto v of his *Orlando Furioso*, first published in 1516; then it was done by Bandello (i, 22) and later by Timoneda (Patraña 19). With Bandello or Ariosto as the source, it appears in Shakespeare's *Much Ado About Nothing* (published in 1600) and in the Spanish play *El desengaño dichoso* (*The Happy Revelation*) by Guillén de Castro (written circa 1599, published in 1621).[3] Final examples from Bandello: Lope de Vega's play *El mayordomo de la duquesa de Amalfi* (1604-1606) and John Webster's *Duchess of Malfi* (1612-1614) have their source in Bandello's Part i, tale 26 (M1508, S105).

The Middle Ages have offered many subjects for later writers. One of the best is the story of Apollonius, Prince of Tyre. The original tale was a Greek romance, no longer extant, dating from the fifth century; a Latin version (*Historia Apollonii Regis Tyri*) is known from the tenth century. The story appears in the *Gesta Romanorum*, compiled about the middle of the fourteenth century, and is number 153 in the modern English edition of Charles Swan. John Gower included it in his *Confessio Amantis* (1383). A Spanish version in 2,624 lines of verse, the *Libro de Apolonio*, dates from the thirteenth century, and a prose version is given by Timoneda (Patraña 11). Although no Spanish play about Apollonius exists, there is the *Comedia de Rubena* by Gil Vicente (1475?-1536?), a Portuguese poet and dramatist, who wrote the play partly in Spanish and partly in Portuguese, basing his plot on a translation of Gower. Then, of course, comes Shake-

---

3 Juan Timoneda, *El patrañuelo*, in Federico Ruiz Morcuende (ed.), *Clásicos castellanos* (Madrid: "La Lectura," 1930), "Prólogo," p. xxvi; Guillén de Castro, *Obras*, Vol. 1, ed. by Eduardo Juliá Martínez (Madrid: Real Academia Española, 1925), lxxxiii; Joanot Martorell, *Tirant lo Blanc*, ed. by Martín de Riquer (Barcelona: Editorial Selecta, 1947), "Introducción, pp. *186-*91.

speare's *Pericles, Prince of Tyre*. Charles Swan, in his notes to
the *Gesta Romanorum*, presents numerous verses from
Shakespeare's play that correspond closely to passages in the
prose account.

The *Sproke van Beatrijs*, a thirteenth-century pious legend
in Flemish, is considered the best version of all the
stories about the nun, Beatrice, who left her convent, ran off
with a lover, and after years of living a sinful life, returned to
the convent to find that her absence had gone unnoticed
because the Virgin Mary, whom she always worshipped, had
taken her place.[4] In its earliest form it is found in *Dialogus
Miraculorum*, written about 1222 by Caesarius von Heister-
bach. The legend is found in Spain as early as the reign of
King Alfonso x, el Sabio (1252-1284) in number 93 of his
Cantigas de Santa María. The legend was dramatized by Lope
de Vega in his play *La buena guarda* (1610), by Pedro Rosete
Niño in his *Sólo en Dios la confianza (Only in God* [One's] *Trust)*
(1662), and told again by José Zorrilla (1817-1893) in his
poetic *leyenda, Margarita la tornera*. The French author
Charles Nodier (1780-1844) wrote *La Légende de Soeur Béatrix*
(1838), and Maurice Maeterlinck a play *Soeur Béatrice* (1901).

Borrowings, lendings, analogues, influences, etc. are not
all in one direction. On the subject of Joan of Arc there is a
Spanish play, *La doncella de Orleans* (published in 1721), by
José de Cañizares and Antonio de Zamora; a German play,
Die Jungfrau von Orleans (1801) by Friedrich Schiller; and in
England, George Bernard Shaw's *Saint Joan* (1924). The
separation of England from the Catholic Church is represented by Shakespeare's *Henry VIII* and the *Cisma de In-
glaterra (The Schism of England)* written by Pedro Calderón de
la Barca (1600-1681) (M2138-39; S171, 300). The tragic fate
of Mary, queen of Scots was recorded for posterity in German in Friedrich Schiller's *Maria Stuart* (1801); *Marie Stuart*,
adapted from Schiller's play by the French dramatist Pierre

---

4   *The Miracle of Beatrice: A Flemish Legend of c. 1300*, English-Flemish
     edition, trans. by Adriaan J. Barnouw, introduction by Jan-Albert
     Goris (New York: Pantheon Books, 1944). Robert Guiette lists over
     200 examples of the legend in many languages in his book *La
     Légende de la Sacristine* (Paris, 1927).

Antoine Lebrun; and *María Estuarda* (1828), a Spanish translation of Lebrun by Manuel Bretón de los Herreros.[5] Two
centuries earlier Spain's greatest dramatist, Lope de Vega,
had chosen to write, not a drama, but an epic poem: *Corona
trágica. Vida y muerte de la Serenissima Reyna de Escocia María
Estuarda* (1627). Pope Urban VIII, to whom it was dedicated,
sent him "a complimentary letter, the title of Doctor of
Theology in the Collegium Sapientiae, and the Cross of the
Order of Saint John."[6]

Spanish drama has had quite an impact on the literatures
of other countries. The protagonist of Tirso de Molina's play
El burlador de Sevilla y convidado de piedra (circa 1630) (*The
Trickster of Seville and Guest of Stone*), Don Juan, has become
known throughout the world. To give just a few examples
out of hundreds, there is, in France, Molière's play *Don Juan,
ou le festin de pierre* (1665), only one of many adaptations. The
Italian playwright Giacinto Andrea Cicognini wrote his play
Il convitato di pietra (circa 1650), based on Tirso de Molina's
(M2855). Among several operas produced during the
eighteenth century, Mozart's *Don Giovanni* (1787) remains
outstanding. Lord Byron treated of him in his poem *Don
Juan* (1819-1824), and in Germany Christian Dietrich Grabbe
composed his drama *Don Juan und Faust* (1829). Back in
Spain José Zorilla wrote his play *Don Juan Tenorio* (1844),
which has been performed annually ever since on November 1, All Saints Day.

Another character who has achieved universal renown is
Don Quixote. Like Minerva from the brow of Jupiter, Don
Quixote was born from the mind of Miguel de Cervantes.
Swaddled in the pages of a novel (Part I, 1605; Part II, 1615),
he grew into more than a hundred plays in Spain alone
(M1355), of which one can represent all—*Don Quixote de la
Mancha*, printed in 1618, by Guillén de Castro (1569-1631).
Jules Massenet, the French composer, wrote an opera, *Don
Quichotte* (1910). Cervantes' novel has been translated into all

5 Mildred Vinson Boyer, *The Texas Collection of 'Comedias sueltas': A
   Descriptive Bibliography* (Boston: G. K. Hall, 1978), 122-23.
6 H. A. Rennert, *The Life of Lope de Vega* (Glasgow, 1904; reprint New
   York: G. E. Stechert, 1937), 324.

modern languages, including Hebrew (the first English
translation was that of Thomas Shelton in 1612), and has
appeared in over seven hundred editions. The name of the
protagonist has entered our language to describe someone
whose behaviour is rather odd—"quixotic." When a person is
considered to be fighting against a presumed injustice or an
imaginary evil or enemy, he is "tilting at windmills," allud-
ing to an incident in the novel.

A third "Don" of Spain led to the production of dramas in
Spain itself and in other countries. The death of prince
Don Carlos (1545-1568), the son of Philip II, under suspicious
circumstances led to many rumours and speculations about
illicit love and murder. Diego Ximénez de Enciso's *El príncipe
don Carlos* and Juan Pérez de Montalbán's *El segundo Séneca
de España y el príncipe don Carlos*, both of uncertain date but
about 1625-1630, are the first dramatic works on the subject.
In France, the Abbé Saint-Réal produced *Don Carlos, nouvelle
historique* (1672), which was one of the sources of Schiller's
German drama *Don Carlos* (1787), and in Italy of Vittorio
Alfieri's *Filippo* (1776). England's Lord John Russell (1792-
1878) also wrote a drama, *Persecution or Don Carlos*. The
libretto of Verdi's opera *Don Carlo* (1867) was based on
Schiller's work. Altogether there have been 105 treatments
of the theme: 30 French, 27 German, 17 English, 13 Italian, 9
Spanish, 8 Dutch, and 1 Portuguese (M994-97). Finally, Gaspar Núñez de Arce (1834-1903), a poet and politician who
served as Colonial Minister under Alfonso XII, wrote *El haz
de leña* (*The Bundle of Kindling*) (1872), considered as "one of
the finest historical dramas of the 19th century" (Encyclo-
pedia Americana).

In addition to works already mentioned, some brief references can be made to foreign adaptations of Spanish dramas
themselves rather than from common sources. In France,
the best known is probably Pierre Corneille's *Le Cid* (1636),
written in the French classical style of five acts of alexandrine
couplets and adapted from Guillén de Castro's *Las mocedades
del Cid* (*The Youthful Deeds of the Cid*), which was done in the
Spanish fashion—three acts of polymetric verse. The play
was first published in 1618 (M2371, 2375-78, 2380, 2387;

S127, 136). Jules Massenet's opera *Le Cid* appeared in 1885. Corneille's play, *Le Menteur*, is based on Juan Ruiz de Alarcón's (1581-1639) *La verdad sospechosa* (*The Truth Suspected*) (M936, 2640; S86, 136). Thomas Corneille used *El alcaide de sí mismo* (*His Own Jailer*) by Pedro Calderón de la Barca for his similarly titled *Le Geôlier de soi même* (1655); and so did Paul Scarron for his play, *Le Gardien de soi même*, of the same year. Molière's *L'Amour médecin* has its source in Lope de Vega's *El acero de Madrid* (M1263, 3579). Jean Rotrou's tragedy, *Saint-Genest, comédien païen représentant le mystère d'Adrien*, comes from Lope de Vega's *Lo fingido verdadero* (*The Make-Believe Come True*) which describes the life and martyrdom of Saint Genesius the Comedian, "an actor at Rome who, while taking part in a burlesque of Christian baptism . . . was suddenly converted and forthwith martyred."[7] This drama contains a play within the play, the device so often pointed out in *Hamlet*. In this regard it may be mentioned that the Spanish dramatist Tamayo y Baus, with *Hamlet* in mind, composed his tragedy, *Un drama nuevo* (1867), in the form of "a play within a play" and included Shakespeare himself as a character (M3154). Rotrou showed his acquaintance with Francisco Rojas Zorrilla (1607-1648) in basing his *Venceslas* on the Spaniard's *No hay ser padre siendo rey* (*A King Cannot Act as a Father*) (M2540, 2551; S256). Another play by Rojas, *Donde hay agravios no hay celos, y amo criado* (*Where There is Dishonor There is No Jealousy, and the Master is the Servant*) is the source of Scarron's *Jodelet, ou le Maître valet*. Thomas Corneille's *Le Feint astrologue* (1648) is derived from Calderón's *El astrólogo fingido* (S298, 339), and his play *Le Comte d'Essex* (1678) comes from *El conde de Sex* by Antonio Coello (1611-1652) (M1059, 2396). Luis Vélez de Guevara (1579-1644) dramatized the legend of Inés de Castro in his *Reinar después de morir* (*To Reign after Death*). Inés has been the mistress, or secretly wedded wife, of crown prince Pedro, son of king Alfonso IV of Portugal. When the king announces that Pedro is to marry Blanca, princess of Navarra, Pedro refuses and says that Inés

---

7 *The Book of Saints*, compiled by the Benedictine monks of St. Augustine's Abbey, Ramsgate (4th ed.; London: Adam and Charles Black, 1947), 257.

de Castro is the one he loves and wants. Inés is murdered by
certain henchmen of the king, and Pedro vows vengeance.
When he succeeds to the throne upon the death of his father
years later, he has the remains of Inés exhumed and placed
upon the throne, where all must kneel and swear allegiance
to her as queen. Henry de Montherlant, the modern French
dramatist, retold the story in his tragedy *La Reine morte*
(1942; English translation *Queen After Death*, 1951) (M898-99;
S296). The English translation of Montherlant's play has
been presented on American television. Many more French
adaptations of Spanish plays can be found in Ernest Mar-
tinenche, *La 'Comedia' espagnole en France de Hardy à Racine*
(Paris, 1900) (M1697; S99).

Rojas, Calderón, and Coello had followers in England.
Rojas' *Donde hay agravios* gave William D'Avenant the plot for
his *The Man's the Master* (M978, S321). Calderón's *El Astrólogo
fingido* led the way to John Dryden's *An Evening's Love, or the
Mock-Astrologer* (S298), and his *Con quien vengo vengo* (*I Come
with the One I Accompany*) provided Dryden with his play *The
Assignation* (M1035, S324). A third play by Calderón, *Mañanas de abril y mayo* (*April and May Mornings*) gave William
Wycherley the material of his *Love in a Wood* (M2090, S325).
Antonio Coello's *El conde de Sex* was the source of two English
plays, John Banks's *The Unhappy Favourite, or the Earl of Essex*
(1682) and Henry Jones's *The Earl of Essex* (1753). Coello's *Los
empeños de seis horas (Six-Hour Engagements)* forms the basis
of Samuel Tuke's *The Adventures of Five Hours* (M2399-
2400).

In Italy Coello's *Conde de Sex* was the source of Niccolò
Biancolelli's *La Regina statista d'Inghilterra ed il Conte di Essex:
vita, successi e morte* (Bologna, 1668). *Las pobrezas de Reinaldos*,
by Lope de Vega, was the inspiration for Giacinto Andrea
Cicognini's *L'Honorata povertà di Rinaldo* and for Carlo Gol-
doni's *Rinaldo di Mont' Albano* (M3407). Calderón's *El mayor
monstro del mundo* gave rise to the Italian play of the same title,
Il maggior mostro del mondo, attributed to Cicognini (M901,
1181-82, 1797), and *El desdén con el desdén* ([Meet] *Disdain with
Disdain*) by Agustín Moreto (1618-1669) became *La Prin-
cipessa filosofa* by Carlo Gozzi (1720-1806) (M1104, 2499).

The Austrian dramatist Franz Grillparzer (1791-1872) was an admirer of Spanish drama and was influenced by Lope de Vega in his *Esther* (Lope's *La hermosa Ester*) (M1060, 1117, 3175) and in his *Die Jüdin von Toledo* (Lope's *Las paces de los reyes y judía de Toledo*) (M1118, 1188-96). Calderón's *La vida es sueño* (*Life is a Dream*) also had its influence, appearing in Grillparzer's *Der Traum, ein Leben*. The German Romantic poet Ludwig Uhlands (1787-1862) made a dramatic sketch or rough draft of a drama, called *Bernardo del Carpio*, based on Lope de Vega's play *El casamiento en la muerte* (*Marriage after Death*), which deals with the legendary Spanish rival of the French Roland, nephew of Charlemagne (M1477, 3503).

Two Spanish dramatists of the nineteenth century produced plays that became operas by Giuseppe Verdi (1813-1901). Angel de Saavedra, Duke of Rivas (1791-1865) wrote the Romantic drama *Don Alvaro, o la fuerza del sino* (1832, performed in 1835), which became Verdi's *La forza del destino* (1862). *El trovador*, by Antonio García Gutiérrez (1813-1884), produced in 1836, was transformed into Verdi's *Il Trovatore*, with its famous "Anvil Chorus" (1853), and his *Simón Bocanegra* (1843) added just one letter to become Verdi's opera *Simon Boccanegra* (1857).

* * * * *

The information provided in the foregoing pages tells us that Spanish drama has dealt with the same topics and themes as the drama of England, France, Germany, and Italy. We are made aware, also, that Spanish literature is not that strange, exotic, half-Oriental thing we had previously believed. As our minds are broadened, we come to realize that, since all those people—Spaniards, Frenchmen, Italians, Germans—write and read about the same things we do, we must all be pretty much alike. Since we have similar tastes, our inability as individuals to understand one another's language is seen as only a minor obstacle to better understanding and friendship. Altogether, these languages and literatures, despite their seeming differences, form part of the motley pattern of West-European culture that is our common heritage. But that is not all; we have taken only a tiny sample from the tip of a very large iceberg.

Who read and compared all those works in several languages and gathered all the information together? It was a cumulative effort on the part of scholars, researchers, students. As a group they may be thought of as workers in the field of literature because they write about writers. But the latter, the creative writers—what do they write about?

At first perusal, the great writers seem to be simply telling stories or describing scenes or events in prose, poetic, or dramatic form. However, once we learn to appreciate such things it becomes clear to us that behind it all they are expressing thought and emotions. When Heinrich Heine (1797-1856) writes

> Du bist wie eine Blume,
> So hold und schön und rein;
> Ich schau dich an, und Wehmut
> Schleicht mir ins Herz hinein[8]

we understand that this sadness is due to his realization that that sweet innocent beauty will not last, but, like the flower, will soon fade and die—as our lives will last but a brief moment on the clock of eternity. William Cullen Bryant (1794-1878) was thinking along the same lines when he wrote, thousands of miles away from Heine,

> Loveliest of lovely things are they,
> On earth, that soonest pass away.
> The rose that lives its little hour
> Is prized beyond the sculptured flower.[9]

Calderón summed it all up in the same terms in his famous sonnet in Act II of *El príncipe constante* (1629):

> Estas, que fueron pompa y alegría
> despertando al albor de la mañana,
> a la tarde serán lástima vana,
> durmiendo en brazos de la noche fría.

---

8   You are just like a flower
               So sweet and fair and pure
               I look at you, and sadness
               Comes creeping into my heart

9   From *A Scene on the Banks of the Hudson.*

Este matiz, que al cielo desafía,
iris listado de oro, nieve y grana,
será escarmiento de la vida humana:
¡tanto se emprende en término de un día!

A florecer las rosas madrugaron
y para envejecerse florecieron:
cuna y sepulcro en un botón hallaron.

Tales los hombres sus fortunas vieron:
en un día nacieron y espiraron;
que pasados los siglos, horas fueron.[10]

Poets, especially, express their ineffable feelings as best they can, by means of words, images, rhythms, rhymes. A young woman looks wide-eyed up at Gustavo Adolfo Bécquer (1836-1870) and asks, "Qué es poesía?" (What is poetry?). He can only reply: "Poesía—eres tú" (Poetry—is you). "To die, to sleep; / To sleep: perchance to dream: ay, there's the rub: / For in that sleep of death what dreams may come. . . ." Shakespeare had a different concept of life and death than did Calderón, who expressed in the form of a play his belief that *La vida es sueño* (*Life is a Dream*).

Not all the great minds and hearts are literary persons. There are philosophers, composers, and artists, as well, and most treat the same things—nature, the universe, life, love, faith, hope, beauty, truth, God. It is as if a great conversation were taking place over the centuries among the great minds—Hegel conversing with Plato, Voltaire with Aristotle,

---

10   A rough translation:

These [flowers] that were so bright and gay,
awaking at the dawn of day,
in the evening will be a sorry sight
sleeping in the arms of the chilly night.

This hue that challenges the sky,
an iris striped with gold, white, and scarlet
will be an example of human life—
so much is undertaken in the space of one day!

The roses got up at dawn to bloom,
and they bloomed only to grow old:
cradle and grave they found in one bud.

Thus did men see their fortunes:
in one day they were born and expired;
after so many centuries they seemed like hours.

Goethe exchanging ideas with Dante, Lope de Vega discussing matters with Ovid and Ariosto, and so on.

All these subjects, these modes of expression—languages, literatures, fine arts, music, philosophy, religious studies—constitute the humanities. They represent the spiritual side of human nature, and embody the beliefs and traditions of the Greco-Roman, Judaeo-Christian culture that we call Western civilization. Without that spirituality we are like animals rooting in the underbrush for sustenance, or like robots toiling mindlessly on an assembly line.

TWO

LOPE DE VEGA: ETERNALLY POPULAR AND MODERN

Jack H. Parker
University of Toronto

> Y escribo por el arte que inventaron
> Los que el vulgar aplauso pretendieron;
> Porque, como las paga el vulgo, es justo
> Hablarle en necio para darle gusto.
> — *Arte nuevo de hacer comedias*
> *en este tiempo* (vv. 45-48)

At first glance this statement of Lope de Vega's seems rude and harsh, as are some other statements to be found in the *Arte nuevo* (1609), in which document Lope appears to be apologizing for his "popularity" and "modernity," as he pours forth his thoughts in the presence of an élite audience made up of members of a Madrid literary circle. Such statements as the above were

19

sufficient to cause Marcelino Menéndez y Pelayo, in *Historia de las ideas estéticas en España*, to brand the *Arte nuevo* as a "lamentable palinodia."[1] This apologetic attitude may be due not to the times, place, or surrounding circumstances, but to literary tradition[2] for it is very clear that one of the strong influences upon Lope de Vega's literary formation was that of the Italian dramatists of the sixteenth century.

As I wrote in 1966, in the Italians' prologues to their *commedie erudite* is to be found, much stronger than any immediate influence, the very wariness which is reflected throughout the *Arte nuevo*. There is no doubt that Lope de Vega knew the Italian dramatists who preceded him, as did his contemporaries in Spain, and in their introductory remarks is found, as a model for him, this same type of apparent apology. The Italians, while stressing their profound admiration for the "classics," refer to the innovations which they deem necessary in the light of the new social order and times. The same caution and prudence is theirs, as is Lope's, as they acknowledge, with questionable sincerity, the indebtedness to the past and the necessity of accepting the modern and the reality of the day. As Juana de José Prades has pointed out in her edition of the *Arte nuevo*, the *vulgo* of whom Lope de Vega seems to be speaking so rudely was a "pueblo capaz de comprender, admirar y seguir representaciones dramáticas—autos, dramas, etc.—llenas de todo género de difíciles conceptos y sutilezas verbales."[3]

This taste of the theatrically-educated *vulgo* must have influenced the content and the course of Lopean drama considerably. For example, José Bergamín has spoken of this "popular" element in "esta comedia española, inventada por Lope de Vega, para el pueblo y por él, en la que ver-

---

1   Marcelino Menéndez y Pelayo, *Historia de las ideas estéticas en España*, Vol. 3 (2nd ed.; Madrid, 1896), 433.

2   See my "Lope de Vega's *Arte nuevo de hacer comedias*: Post-Centenary Reflections," in John Esten Keller and Karl-Ludwig Selig (eds.), *Hispanic Studies in Honor of Nicholson B. Adams* (Chapel Hill, North Carolina, 1966), 113-30.

3   Lope de Vega, *Arte nuevo*, ed. by Juana de José Prades (Madrid, 1971), 51.

daderamente se entera España de sí misma: porque entera y verdaderamente se populariza por ella. . . ."[4]

The very "popular" in all of the *comedia lopesca*, whether in the case of Lope de Vega himself or in the case of his contemporaries and followers, is surely to be found above all in the cloak and sword plays—those delightful dramas which are closest to the people, and likewise the most modern of them all, in the sense that they deal with universal human emotions and interests, true in Lope de Vega's time and also in the twentieth century.

In an essay written apparently some forty years ago, but not published (posthumously) until 1980, the late Edward M. Wilson has given a good account of Calderón's contribution to the genre.[5] And several other critics, such as Bruce W. Wardropper, have pointed out the importance and richness of these *capa y espada* plays as an important part of Siglo de Oro theatre.[6] These very entertaining pieces may appear, at least on the surface, more frivolous than the "deeper" dramas. Yet within them are to be found the usual serious *comedia* themes of love and honour, and a philosophy of life which is not the "hollow philosophy" that William Atkinson believed he could observe in a Calderón de la Barca play such as *No hay burlas con el amor*.[7] In the *comedias de capa y espada* there is, on the contrary, a very serious note, as Wardropper has pointed out. And even Lope de Vega, said to be less subtle than Calderón, presents to us in his cloak and sword plays "the confusion of the World," wherein "men are deceived by their senses" (Wilson, p. 95).

---

4   José Bergamín, *Mangas y capirotes: España en su laberinto teatral del XVII* (Madrid, 1933), 32-33.

5   "The Cloak and Sword Plays," in D. W. Cruickshank (ed.), *Spanish and English Literature of the 16th and 17th Centuries. Studies in Discretion, Illusion and Mutability* (Cambridge, 1980), 90-104.

6   Bruce W. Wardropper, "Calderón's Comedy and his Serious Sense of Life," in Keller and Selig (eds.), *Hispanic Studies*, 179-93; and Bruce W. Wardropper, "El problema de la responsabilidad en la comedia de capa y espada de Calderón," *Actas del Segundo Congreso Internacional de Hispanistas* (Nijmegen, 1967), 689-94.

7   William Atkinson, "Studies in Literary Decadence. II. La comedia de capa y espada," *Bulletin of Hispanic Studies* 4 (1927), 80-89.

One of Lope de Vega's best *capa y espada* plays, *Amar sin saber a quién*, raises a question which enters into the realm of modern psychology: is it possible to fall in love with an unknown person? Macías, in Lope de Vega's *Porfiar hasta morir*, it is true, falls in love with Clara even before knowing the lady's name (Macías: "Decidme / vuestro nombre ..." [1]). Our jailed Don Fernando, of *Amar sin saber a quién*, needs nothing more than a written note from an unknown *dama* to fall head over heels. The two hundred *escudos* accompanying the communication and a later small portrait bring the enamourment to fruition. In these two cases, and in so many others, Lope de Vega is portraying human nature of any century, to the extent of having the more down-to-earth *gracioso* of *Porfiar hasta morir*, Nuño, aghast at such speed in falling in love. Macías' remark is "¡Qué gran belleza!"; Nuño's retort in reply is "¡Qué gran necedad!" (1). And Macías, poet, is reminded by his servant that "La locura y la poesía / de una manera se hallan":

> [Nuño] Hace un hombre cuando mozo
> dos romances a su dama,
> de allí se pasa a un soneto,
> luego a una canción se pasa,
> luego a un libro de pastores,
> y cuando ya tiene fama,
> y es declarado poeta
> (que no es pequeña desgracia),
> dice que es Virgilio, Homero,
> desprecia con arrogancia
> a todos cuantos escriben;
> y de aquesta misma traza
> es un loco. ...   (1)

La dama boba, to cite another example of Lope de Vega's modern approach to life, is an excellent study of human psychology in any age. Joseph G. Fucilla has shown that our dramatist's presentation is very much twentieth-century and up to date.[8] Overshadowed by her "clever" sister, Nise, Finea enters into the action of the play revealing a psychopathic

---

8   Joseph G. Fucilla, "Finea in Lope's *La dama boba* in the Light of Modern Psychology," *Bulletin of the Comediantes* 7 (1955), 22-23.

feeblemindedness, which is in due course overcome and cured by the attention paid to her by young Laurencio. "It is surprising," wrote Fucilla, "that Lope more than three hundred years ago had anticipated in his play some of the most recent findings of our psychology specialists" (p. 23). Yet it is not so surprising when we are reminded by Fucilla (note 1) that "the motif of an I.Q. increase through love had currency long before Lope's time"; not so surprising either when we remember that the very modern ruse of "defensive stupidity" is used by this very same Finea to avoid marrying an unwanted suitor, Liseo, and to keep Laurencio. This "defence" is also used by another Lopean heroine, Diana, with all her faculties intact, in *La boba para los otros y discreta para sí*.

This very modernity on Lope's part is due to his keen perception of human nature, and his observation of society round about him was much used in his plays. Lope de Vega's life was comparatively long, and his contacts with fellow human beings, especially women, were continuous. He was not aloof in an ivory tower writing of theoretical actions and reactions. On the contrary, he could see logically the conflicts going on in humanity in the seventeenth century in Spain; conflicts which are not much different nowadays, though in a period, perhaps, of more subtleties and technological advances. Writing of *La discreta enamorada*, Myron A. Peyton reminds us that the life of Madrid was much used by Lope in his plays, and that "Life in Lope's time was in crisis."[9]

Great changes were taking place in the areas of human consciousness. Some of these developments became important features of the *comedia* as we know it: the dignity of the person . . . ; the inevitable conflict between the individual and the social principles and institutions within which his existence took place; a growing scepticism regarding tradition and its formulations, with a realistic appraisal of social systems and abstractions of all sorts; a consequent realignment of human values; a widened range of choice of belief and action, with some confusion of alternatives confronting the individual. . . . This was the world Lope himself experienced, and it

---

9 Myron A. Peyton, "*La discreta enamorada* as an Example of Dimensional Development in the *Comedia*," *Hispania* 40 (1957), 162.

is this life, in substance and detail, which he re-created in his dramas (p. 162).

Whatever source materials Lope de Vega put his hand on, he developed his plays generally speaking "in the dimensions of his own society, whose widening consciousness his artist's genius was able to perceive and interpret to it" (ibid.).

If we look at each of Peyton's phrases about Lope de Vega, it seems clear enough that 1982 presents a world not too different in its social problems from 1606 or 1620-1622.[10] Man is still striving "to become something more than himself" (ibid.), the individual still has his or her conflicts with twentieth-century society, and we have a continuing scepticism about formerly accepted values and a realignment of those values. We have, in addition, the same psychological questions and answers before us which Lope de Vega portrayed so well in *La dama boba* or in *Amar sin saber a quién*.

Amar sin saber a quién, to go back to that "popular" and "modern" play, is particularly pertinent to this volume in honour of Dr. Neale H. Tayler, because a distinguished Canadian under whom President Tayler studied in his youth edited that play many years ago and mentioned the play so many times in his classes at the University of Toronto. I refer, of course, to the Milton A. Buchanan edition of *Amar sin saber a quién* of 1920.[11] For Buchanan, *Amar sin saber a quién* was a prime favorite, and "a typical cloak and sword, *capa y espada* comedy" (Preface) in which Spain's old capital, Toledo, is given much importance. In fact, Lope de Vega was very fond of Toledo, and it is likely that he was in that city when he wrote the play. So important indeed was Toledo in Lope's mind and affection that he reminds us, in the words of Don Fernando, that

> Dicen que una ley dispone
> que si acaso se levanta

---

10   Dates given by the Morley and Bruerton, *Cronología de las comedias de Lope de Vega* (Madrid, 1968), for *La discreta enamorada* and *Amar sin saber a quién*, respectively.
11   Milton A. Buchanan and Bernard Franzén-Swedelius (eds.), *Amar sin saber a quién* (New York, 1920).

> sobre un vocablo porfía
> de la lengua castellana,
> lo juzgue el que es de Toledo.   (1)

This old "law," it is said, went back to the time of Alfonso el Sabio in the mid-thirteenth century; and the old *questione della lingua* (which so much preoccupied the Italians, for example, and Frenchmen like Du Bellay in his *Défense et illustration de la langue française*) was on the minds of many in Lope de Vega's time, from Melchor de Santa Cruz (*Floresta de apothegmas y sentencias*, Toledo, 1574) to Sancho Panza: "Sí, que ¡válgame Dios! no hay para qué obligar al sayagués a que hable como el toledano..." (*Don Quijote*, II, xix). And, adds Don Fernando of *Amar sin saber a quién*,

> Y que otra ley promulgaba
> que en hablando de hermosura
> que entendimiento acompaña,
> sólo juzgarlo pudiera
> una dama toledana.

So, according to our Lope play, the Toledans had the authority for both language and feminine beauty!

Melchor de Santa Cruz, who spent the last of his life in Toledo, went to great lengths to stress the superior language of that city: "esta antigua y noble ciudad de Toledo ... donde todo el primor y elegancia del bien decir florece" (in the dedication of his book to Don Juan de Austria). In his *Floresta* he goes on to explain the why and wherefore of the city's language position:

En lo que toca al estilo y propiedad con que se debe escribir, una cosa no me puede dejar de favorecer; y es el lugar donde lo escribo, cuya autoridad en las cosas que toca al común hablar es tanta, que las leyes del Reino disponen que cuando en alguna parte se dudare de algún vocablo castellano, lo determine el hombre toledano que allí se hallare. Lo cual por justas causas se mandó juntamente: La primera porque esta ciudad está en el centro de toda España, donde es necesario que, como en el corazón se producen más subtiles espíritus, por la sangre más delicada que allí se envía, así también en el pueblo que es el corazón de alguna región está la habla y la conversación más aprobada que en otra parte de aquel reino.

La segunda, por estar lejos del mar, no hay ocasión, por causa del puerto, a que gentes extranjeras hayan de hacer mucha morada en él; de donde se sigue corrupción de la lengua, y aun también de las costumbres.

La tercera, por la habilidad y buen ingenio de los moradores que en ella hay; los cuales, o porque el aire con que respiran es delgado, o porque el clima y constelación les ayuda, o porque ha sido lugar donde los Reyes han residido, están tan despiertos para notar cualquiera impropiedad que se hable, que no es menester se descuide el que con ellos quisiere tratar de esto ... (*Floresta*, 1574, *dedicatoria*).

Marcelino Menéndez y Pelayo speaks of "esta fantástica ley tan traída y llevada por nuestros antiguos escritores," and doubts that such a law really existed.[12] He believes that the tradition may have arisen from an erroneous interpretation of a clause in the *Fuero general de Toledo*. Alfred Morel-Fatio, in France, had picked up this old idea too and had commented on it:

Tolède, nous dit-on, est l'école du parler pur: elle règle l'usage, et cela en vertu d'un acte royal. Alphonse x, aux cortes tenues à Tolède en 1253, déclare et ordonne que 'toutes les fois qu'une contestation s'élèvera sur l'acceptation d'un mot castillan, il faudra recourir à Tolède, mètre de la langue castillane, et accepter celle que lui reconnaîtront les habitants de cette ville.'[13]

Morel-Fatio, like Menéndez y Pelayo, had no proof of the certain existence of any such law, and for "cette croyance générale en un acte du pouvoir royal" (p. 177), he quotes several "authorities" who mention a "law," such as Francisco de Pisa, *Descripción de la imperial ciudad de Toledo* (Toledo, 1605) and Gonzalo Fernández de Oviedo, *Las quinquagenas de la nobleza de España* ı (Madrid, 1880). From the beginning of the sixteenth century, Toledo was the usual place of residence of the King, and therefore the language of Toledo "équivaut à langage parlé à la cour" (Morel-Fatio, p. 178). The speech of Toledo was held in high esteem by many men of letters of the Golden Age. For example, Juan de Valdés, in his *Diálogo de la lengua*, writes: "como a hombre criado en el

---

12   Marcelino Menéndez y Pelayo, *Orígenes de la novela*, Vol. 2 (Madrid, 1907), lxvi, note.

13   Alfred Morel-Fatio, *Ambrosio de Salazar et l'étude de l'espagnol en France sous Louis XIII* (Paris, 1900), 176, quoting from Francisco de Pisa, *Descripción de la imperial ciudad de Toledo* (Toledo, 1605).

reino de Toledo y en la corte de España, os preguntaremos de la lengua que se usa en la corte"; Cervantes, in addition to the above-mentioned declaration of Sancho Panza, pays tribute to Toledo's language also in *El viaje del Parnaso* VI: "En propio toledano y buen romance les dio los buenos días cortésmente"; and Gracián, in *El criticón* II, speaks of Toledo as "la escuela del bien hablar."

But as Valladolid and then Madrid gained the ascendancy as the court cities, Toledo's authority declined and the others rose in prominence as the models of elegance in language.

It is Carmen Bravo-Villasante of *La mujer vestida de hombre* fame who has paid special attention to *Amar sin saber a quién*. In a seminal article and in her later edition of the play she has pointed to the interesting psychological study which is before us.[14] Let me stress again: Lope de Vega is entirely twentieth-century (as well as seventeenth) in his approach to human nature; his treatment of human behaviour is as relevant as the common manifestations of psychological problems one reads about in modern-day newspapers and magazines. This "enamorarse de un retrato, enamorarse de oídas" was common in old times also, whether it was a case of Spanish or other literatures such as the Italian *Il Cortegiano*, where one finds "el caso de un caballero del que se enamoran muchas damas, sin conocerle, sólo porque oyeron alabanzas du su persona en boca de otra dama." For "la fama de sus virtudes y de su nobleza fue transmitiéndose de unas a otras, y así él, sin saberlo, tuvo rendidos muchos corazones" (Bravo-Villasante, p. 195).

It is possible, or even probable, that this process of receiving "un flechazo sin conocer al ser amado" had something to do with courtly love and its exaggerated chivalrous cult. As Carmen Bravo-Villasante writes correctly, "el teatro español, que en muchos aspectos vivía del ideal caballeresco, acogió con agrado estas formas literarias de enamorarse. . . . El se encargaba de presentarlas al público de manera que no se dudase de su verosimilitud."

---

14 Carmen Bravo-Villasante, "Un debate amoroso: *Amar sin saber a quién*," *Revista de Literatura* 7 (1955), 193-99; and her edition of the play, *Amar sin saber a quién* (Salamanca, 1967) (Biblioteca Anaya, 81).

The characters of a play, of course, often debate the possibilities and probabilities of the psychological cause and effect. *Amar sin saber a quién*'s *gracioso*, Limón, brings forth a frequently held opinion of philosophers:

> Los filósofos dijeron
> que no puede haber amor
> donde no hay conocimiento;

and Isabel, of Rojas Zorrilla's *Entre bobos anda el juego*, insists that

> No entra amor tan de repente
> por la vista; amor se engendra
> del trato. . . .

To this Don Pedro retorts:

> . . . más se entiende
> que amor puede haber sin trato.

Carmen Bravo-Villasante has gathered together a large number of examples in *comedias* and in other works of literature, noting that the cold, reasoning eighteenth-century critics, including Luzán in his *Poética*, found fault with this enamourment. Nevertheless, Clavela, of Francisco Salado Garcés' *A lo que obliga el desdén*, holds the dominant point of view:

> Yo amo sin saber a quién,
> Yo doy suspiros al aire
> sin saber a quién se dan.

And Bravo-Villasante has the final word: "Con burla o sin burla, tengan razón unos u otros, el caso es que el tema de 'amar sin saber a quién' encuentra acogida en muchas comedias del teatro del siglo de oro y da lugar a bellas disquiciones conceptistas muy del agrado del público, acostumbrado a estos debates amorosos" (p. 199).

There is no doubt that in the *Comedia* of the Golden Age there is reflected in great measure, although sometimes idealized, the society of the day. Lope de Vega's *Arte nuevo de hacer comedias en este tiempo* had used, regarding this very point, some words which are almost a literal translation of Robortello:

> Ya tiene la Comedia verdadera
> Su fin propuesto, como todo género
> De poema o poesis, y éste ha sido
> Imitar las acciones de los hombres
> Y pintar de aquel siglo las costumbres (vv. 49-53).[15]

Also, the Duque, in Lope de Vega's *El castigo sin venganza*, makes the following statement on the subject:

> ¿Ahora sabes, Ricardo,
> que es la comedia un espejo
> en que el necio, el sabio, el viejo
> . . . .
> retrata nuestras costumbres. . . ?   (i)

In addition to being influenced by customs in general, the *Comedia* also reflected past history and legend and the occasional current event.[16] For example, *La moza de cántaro*'s "soneto a la venida del inglés a Cádiz," as a contemporary happening, referred to the English attack on Cádiz in October, 1625. Also, Act ii of the play makes use of Luis de Góngora's "Alegoría de la brevedad de las cosas humanas":

> Aprended, flores, de mí
> Lo que va de ayer a hoy;
> Que ayer maravilla fui,
> Y hoy sombra mía aun no soy.

This poem, no doubt, had a wide circulation in Lope de Vega's lifetime.

A picturesque fact of nature often added a colourful touch in a character's speech:

---

15   Francesco Robortello, "Finem habet sibi propositum comoedia eum, quem et alia poëmatum genera, imitari mores et actiones hominum" (*Explicatio eorum omnium quae ad Comoedia artificium pertinent*, 1555).

16   "Customs" and the use of "society" in the *Comedia* have a rich bibliography. Some articles are: C. E. Anibal, "The Historical Elements of Lope de Vega's *Fuente Ovejuna*," *Publications of the Modern Language Association of America* 44 (1934), 657-718; G. I. Dale, "'Periodismo' in *El arenal de Sevilla* and the Date of the Play's Composition," *Hispanic Review* 8 (1940), 18-23 [reference to contemporary political figures, including a new general, the Conde de Niebla]; Ruth L. Kennedy, "*La prudencia en la mujer* and the Ambient that Brought it Forth," *Publications of the Modern Language Association of America* 63 (1948), 1131-90; and the monumental book by Ricardo del Arco y Garay, *La sociedad española en las obras dramáticas de Lope de Vega* (Madrid, 1942).

> Cuando el madroño sangriento
> su verde fruta colora,
> salir de sus altas cuevas
> los osos peludos osan.

Here, in *Los Tellos de Meneses*, Act II, Mendo is describing an
annual event which is represented on the coat of arms of the
City of Madrid: the bears' attempting to reach, and eat, the
ripe fruit of the strawberry tree. Current practices, such as
the common laundry described in *La moza de cántaro*, III, also
often make their way into *comedias*.

On the other side, however, to what extent and how did
the *Comedia* in general influence seventeenth-century society? That is a matter much harder to assess. Lope de Vega
was not a moralist. He would not go beyond holding an
example before the eyes, his *ensalzar deleitando*. Some other
dramatists, of course, were preachers and teachers. Tirso de
Molina's *El Burlador de Sevilla* was probably intended to
condemn the immoralities of some members of society and
to show and remind the audience that God's judgment and
punishment (or reward) were not far off. Ruiz de Alarcón's
moralistic plays, such as *La verdad sospechosa* and *Las paredes
oyen*, pointed to the destructive results of man's foibles, in
these cases, lying and gossipping. The "bad man" in each
play lost out, but it is difficult to ascertain how seriously the
audience took the message and what lasting impact the "lesson" really had. The *autos sacramentales*, put on in the public
square for Corpus Christi celebrations, were surely sermons
in dramatic form, and must have had a considerable influence on those assembled. In addition, Joseph H. Silverman, a
few years ago, argued that Lope de Vega's *La mayor virtud de
un rey* (for Silverman Lope's last play) was a direct message
and plea to King Philip IV to administer justice impartially
and democratically as well as a plea to the seducer-abductor
Cristóbal Tenorio, who had run off with, and later abandoned, Lope's daughter Antonia Clara in 1634.[17] Philip IV
had apparently "turned a deaf ear to Lope's pleas against

---

17   Joseph H. Silverman, "Lope de Vega's Last Years and His Final Play,
     The Greatest Virtue of a King," *The Texas Quarterly* 6 (1963), 174-87.

Cristóbal Tenorio," and Silverman feels that the play may have been Lope's "last, desperate attempt to persuade Tenorio to marry Antonia Clara." If this be so, Lope de Vega did not succeed in his endeavour; he was only able to use a fictional, utopian play-dénouement to assuage his wounded soul. In short, in Silverman's words, "Lope, with his unflagging optimism, knew how to transmute the bitterness and disenchantments of reality into the pure gold of an exultant, exemplary, lyrical and ethical sublimation of life in seventeenth-century Spain. In this way he achieved an equilibrium for his tortured soul and a source of unmatched pleasure for his audience."

"The emblematists," Robert J. Clements has written of the Renaissance, "saw the theatre as a medium for correcting society and making people better, [and] they appropriated to their own emblem books the function of 'theater.'"[18] In the late nineteenth century, Strindberg continued the same idea: "Theatre has long seemed to me . . . a *Biblia pauperum*, a Bible in pictures for those who cannot read what is written or printed" (Preface to *Miss Julie*, 1888). Indeed, many critics stress the visual and pictorial character of theatre as a teaching and learning process. In the Spanish Golden Age, with so many illiterates devoted to hearing and seeing their entertainment and moral instruction, the fall and salvation of Julia in Calderón's *La devoción de la cruz*, for example, or the "hundimiento del sepulcro, con mucho ruido" at the end of *El Burlador de Sevilla*, could not have passed unnoticed. Again, to what extent would the "lesson" be a lasting one? The people had these "influences" before them, to accept or to reject. The approach of the Spanish dramatists of the seventeenth century was a "popular" one; the psychology of the plays could belong to any generation.

Writing about Calderón de la Barca—and she could have been writing just as well about Lope de Vega or the other dramatists too—Micheline Sauvage, in her turn, has given emphasis to the "popular" element to be found in the theatre of the Golden Age:

---

18   Robert J. Clements, *Picta poesis: Literary and Humanistic Theory in Renaissance Emblem Books* (Rome, 1960), 190.

Par (et non malgré) sa forme poétique ce théâtre est un théâtre populaire. La pièce à l'usage des lettrés ou des gens de goût n'existe pas. La pâture scénique proposée à l'appétit du Prince est la même que celle de ses plus humbles sujets. . . . Or il est, ce public, extrêmement mêlé. Dans l'enceinte des *corrales* il y a prêtres et laïcs, nobles et gens de peu. Si les "baignoires" élégantes coûtent le prix prohibitif de dix-sept réaux et demi, il n'en coûte que monnaie de billon pour accéder au parterre et y voir le spectacle debout.[19]

This democratic dramatic situation is particularly true of Lope de Vega, farther from the Court than many and very "popular" and "modern" in his treatments and interpretations. About him Sauvage has pointed out "la conformité entre l'art du dramaturge et la société où il parut" (p. 68). He was popular in the most positive of senses, and he is modern in the framework of continuing human psychology. One can in conclusion insist that Lope de Vega is indeed eternally popular and modern.

---

19   Micheline Sauvage, *Calderón: Dramaturge* (Paris, 1959), 18.

THREE

REFLECTIONS OF REALITY

T. B. Barclay
University of Toronto

The Spanish theatre in almost every stage of its development reflects the manners, speech, fads, foibles, and fancies of the current period. That this is so is due to the fact that it is basically a popular theatre.It reflects the tastes of the average theatre-goer, his nature and character in its strength and weakness. There are two comparatively short-lived exceptions to this general statement, one in the eighteenth century and one in the nineteenth. The two exceptions, although in most respects diametrically opposed, have a common characteristic. In each case, dramatic writers are drawn, for various seemingly compelling reasons, to imitate a foreign artistic formula. To reinforce the common bond, in each case the magnetic force is French. With that, however, all similarities cease. The eighteenth-century fashionable writer is following a pattern, a code, a formal

model. The nineteenth-century playwright in the Romantic
period, between 1833 and approximately 1850, is concerned
with the abandonment of purity of form to achieve a spirit of
freedom and individualism. It must be stated again, however, that neither of these two periods is indicative of a
change of personality in the Spanish people. Eighteenth-
century neoclassicism was never intended for, nor ever accepted by, the average audience. The imitation of French
classicism was, first, a reaction to excesses in the national
drama, and second, an attempt to fall in with the fashions of a
French-oriented court. In the nineteenth century, it was a
reaction to excessive political authoritarianism, and although
this time the plays were received with enthusiasm, there was
again no attempt to identify with contemporary life, for the
medieval backgrounds were almost as remote as the
Graeco-Roman models of the neoclassicists had been.

Not all eighteenth-century literature, though, was content
to look back, or, for that matter, to look anywhere but at life
as it was being lived at the moment. It is in comedy, specifically in the delicious tidbit or *sainete*, that this is most evident.

The finest exponent of the *sainete* form is Ramón de la
Cruz who prided himself on holding a mirror to the life of his
times:

Los que han paseado el día de San Isidro su pradera; los que han
visto el Rastro por la mañana, la Plaza mayor de Madrid la víspera
de Navidad, el Prado antiguo por la noche, y han velado en las de
San Juan y San Pedro; los que han asistido a los bailes de todas
clases de gentes y destinos; los que visitan por ociosidad, por vicio o
por ceremonia. . . . En una palabra, cuantos han visto mis sainetes
reducidos al corto espacio de veinte y cinco minutos de repre-
sentación, . . . digan si son copias o no de lo que ven sus ojos y de lo
que oyen sus oídos; si los planes están o no arreglados al terreno
que pisan; y si los cuadros no representan la historia de nuestro
siglo.[1]

As had become traditional, the typical Madrilenian's first
recourse for entertainment is to the theatre, but, lacking this,
there are other possibilities as can be seen from this inter-

---

1   Ramón de la Cruz, *Colección de sainetes*, Vol. 1, ed. by Durán (Madrid,
    1843), xl.

change between Anselmo and Teodoro meeting on Christmas Eve at the beginning of *La Plaza Mayor*:

ANSELMO: ... como no hay comedias,
            pensando iba en qué pasar
            la tarde.

TEODORO: ¡Gentil simpleza!
            Hombre, pues ¿hay tarde alguna
            tan divertida como ésta,
            yendo á la Plaza Mayor?[2]

On their way they meet various types, each of whom reveals something of the temper of the times. First is the maidservant who has been making some profitable visits. The mistress of one house has gone out:

                pero el amo, que me aprecia
                me ha regalado tres libras
                de chocolate, unas velas
                de cera, dos pesos gordos,
                y una caja de jalea.[3]

It is significant that she intends to spend the money thus acquired not on essentials but on what will make a brave outward show:

                Tenga una muger buen guante,
                buen zapato, buena media,
                mantilla limpia y basquiña
                bien plegada y algo estrecha,
                que en la calle solo luce
                lo que se vé por de fuera.[4]

Next is D. Petardo who voices the eternal lament of students down the ages. Others of less ability prosper, meanwhile he starves:

                ¡Que haya quien se dé a las letras
                y no se dé á los arbitrios,
                sabiendo cuanto granjea
                mas que aquél, porque merece,
                el otro porque se ingenia![5]

---

2 Ibid., Vol. 2, 464.
3 Ibid., 465.
4 Ibid.
5 Ibid.

Off he goes to the Plaza:

> a satisfacer en ella
> el hambre de olfato y vista,
> ya que el gusto lo carezca.[6]

The extravagance of entertaining is exemplified by the poor husband, D. Antonio, who on the insistence of his wife empties his pockets and fills his baskets in the Plaza. Anselmo comments:

> el que llena en la Plaza
> esta tarde cuatro espuertas,
> y á su tertulia le da
> un baile en carnestolendas,
> con lo que le sobra este año
> no hará el que viene la fiesta.[7]

The *beata*, fallen on evil days, remembers better times of feasting and music and instructs her little daughter to weep and cry to excite the charity of anyone they may meet in the market.

There are also, of course, the figures peculiar to the time, the *majo* and *maja*, for example, preparing to attend "la misa del Gallo," after which, no doubt, as was the custom, they will patrol the streets beating drums and singing at the pitch of their voices. Likewise the *petimetre* and *petimetra* make their appearance, in this case, D. Antonio's pretentious wife and her lover.

All these typical figures of the day are displayed against an equally realistic background. It may be, as in the cases cited above, the market square with the vendors hawking their wares, customers haggling over prices or seeking to ingratiate themselves with wealthier neighbours in the hope of an invitation to dinner, or even, as the playlet's noisy ending reveals, stealing from the booths.

One of the favourite places for recreation in Madrid was the Ermita de San Isidro del Campo, southwest of the city on the west bank of the Manzanaeres. During the latter half of May this was the scene of pilgrimage, not so much in homage

---

6   Ibid., 466.
7   Ibid., 467.

to Madrid's patron saint, San Isidro, but rather for purposes of eating and drinking, flirtation, and dancing. The setting is described by Ramón de la Cruz in *La Pradera de San Isidro*:

... se descubre la ermita de San Isidro en el foro, sirviendo el tablado á la imitación propia de la Pradera, con bastidor de selva, y algunos árboles repartidos, á cuyo pie estarán diferentes ranchos de personas, de esta suerte: de dos árboles grandes que habrá al medio del tablado: al pie del uno, sobre una capa tendida, estarán JUAN y LORENZO, la NICASIA y la CASILDA, de payas, merendando, con un burro en pelo al lado, y un chiquillo de teta sobre el albardon sirviéndole de cuna, y le mece JUAN cuando llore. Al pie de otro estarán bailando seguidillas, la MANUELA y la ISIDRA con ESTEBAN y RAFAEL, de majos ordinarios de trueno, y la JOAQUINA. Al primer bastidor se sentará NICOLÁS solo sobre su capa, y sacará su cazuela, rábanos, cebolla grande, lechugas etc., y hará su ensalada sin hablar, y al de enfrente estará arrimado CALDERON, de capa, gorro y bastón, con una rica chupa, como atisvando las mozas; seis ú ocho muchachos cruzarán la escena con cántaros de agua, vasos, y ramos de álamo; y al pie del telón en que está figurada la ermita se verá el paseo de los coches, y á un lado un despeñadero en que rueden otros muchachos. GERTRUDIS y VICENTA se pasean vendiendo tostones y ramilletes.[8]

The *seguidilla* sung and danced here has what might be termed a descant in the form of a howling infant and a braying ass:

> El señor San Isidro
> nos ha enviado
> porque le celebremos
> un día claro.[9]

Not only is the writer's gift of humour evident in these scenes—such as servants, forbidden to leave the house, but who succeed in doing so by disguising themselves in their employers' clothes—but there are many penetrating glances at the slyness of lackeys in lining their own pockets. Tailors dress themselves out of the material ordered by their customers. Coachmen pad their expense accounts by increasing the amounts charged on coach upkeep.

In addition to humour, song and dance, so essential to the Spanish character, are neatly inserted into the fabric of

---

8 Ibid., Vol. 1, 224.
9 Ibid.

the plays. It may be a *jácara* sung by blind beggars in the square in the hope of an *aguinaldo*, or it may be dances to the accompaniment of tambourine or guitar, as part of a holiday celebration. For the opening scene of *Manolo* there is a musical background provided by the Galician bagpipes. Occasionally music provides a comic effect: in this play there is the sound of cowbells offstage, and Mediodiente asks,

> ¿ . . . qué salva
> de armonía bestial el aire llena?[10]

The lyrics of a song may be adapted to the situation as, for instance, Pintorilla incorporates an invitation to buy her chestnuts into the *seguidilla* she is singing in *Las castañeras picadas*:

> A mis castañas
> que en Madrid no se comen
> más resaladas.[11]

One of the popular rhythms of the time, the *bolero*, is indicated by the same character in another *seguidilla*:

> A bailar el bolero
> y asar castañas. . . .[12]

The lively *fandango*, another popular measure of the period, is also mentioned in *Las castañeras picadas* as El Macareno orders Pintorilla:

> . . . recoge la mantilla
> y ve á buscar á tu hermana,
> que te espera para ir
> al fandango de la Paca. . . .[13]

The party alluded to turns out to be a rather elaborate affair—*boleros* are danced to the accompaniment of guitar, bandore, violin and castanets. The bandore, a small guitar, is presumably referred to later by Gorito as a *tiple*:

---

10   Ibid., 483.
11   Ibid., Vol. 2, 173.
12   Ibid., 176.
13   Ibid., 180.

> ¿Han venido mis amigos,
> los del tiple, la guitarra
> y el vigolín[14] [vigolín here equals violín].

The same instrument is referred to slightingly by Juana in *La Petra y la Juana*:

> ... tan en cueros
> naturales, que no tiene
> la víspera de San Pedro
> para pagar una mala
> bandurria, ó un par de ciegos.[15]

The pretentiousness of the *petimetres* is mocked in *Las castañeras picadas*, as, to the rhythm of a *bolero*, they position themselves for a minuet:

> Luis
> Toquen minuet.
>   Músicos
>   No sabemos.
>   Vecina 1ª.
> ¡Esta es mucha bufonada,
> que nosotras no bailamos
> sino minué y contradanzas![16]

Ramón de la Cruz is, of course, here referring to the aping of French manners by some of his countrymen who would consider the *menuet* and *contredanse* more refined than the native measures.

It is worth noting that these imports are derided by the onlookers who proceed to dance *seguidillas boleras* and that this play ends with Estefanía singing a traditional *tirana*. Nevertheless, it is a *contredanse* that occurs at the end of *La Petra y la Juana* as the tailor sings: "Y concluirá el argumento / de la Petra y de la Juana...."[17] This immediately precedes the deafening final chorus sung to the accompaniment of bugles and kettledrums.

Even the adherents of traditional rhythms, however, were sometimes divided into rival factions. This is nicely indicated by the lyrics sung at the beginning of *La Petra y la Juana*:

---

14   Ibid., 183.
15   Ibid., 280.
16   Ibid., 186.
17   Ibid., 290.

Vale una seguidilla
de las manchegas
por veinte y cinco pares
de las boleras.[18]

It was toward the middle of the eighteenth century that the
term *boleras* was being used for *seguidillas*. The *seguidillas*
from La Mancha referred to here had a special tune and
were in three-eighths time.

La Petra y la Juana takes place during the last days of June
when Saint John's Eve (June 23) and Saint Peter's (June 29)
provide an occasion for dancing and song. Here a tailor and
his wife sing a *jota* which is clearly identified in the words as a
tirana:"Ésta sí que es tira-tirana...."[19] This is quickly followed by another sung by the same couple containing an
identical line. The instruments are specified with which the
neighbours deafen the district in the celebration of the feast
days:

El Moreno

Mira, he topado al maestro
de capilla de los niños
dotrinos, que tiene un yerno
que toca la chirimia
como un clarinete.

. . . .

Dice que él traerá un bajon
y un bajoncillo, lo mesmo
que un órgano. Que tambien
vendrá su vecino el ciego
con la gaita zamorana....

. . . .

Y se me da
mi camarada el sargento
de Suizos el tamboron
de la retreta, yo apuesto
á que aturdimos el barrio,
y á que no se da en el reino
otra música como ella
esta noche de San Pedro.[20]

---

18   Ibid., 273.
19   Ibid., 274.
20   Ibid., 275.

In contrast, two blind men sing to the accompaniment only
of a violin and tambourine:

> De San Juan en las noches
> y de San Pedro
> no hace mal á las damas
> nunca el sereno.[21]

The *gaita zamorana* deserves specific mention. This is a
stringed instrument of the violin type. To quote Percy A.
Scholes, "it is played by turning with the right hand a handle
which operates a rosined wheel (a circular bow) and by depressing with the left hand a few finger-keys like those of the
piano. The latter operates an internal mechanism function-
ing somewhat like the fingers of the left hand of a violinist."[22]
It is, in fact, the hurdy-gurdy or *lira organizzata*, the favourite
instrument of the poor *lazzaroni* of Naples. The hurdy-
gurdy was once a highly respected instrument and was even
played in churches. King Ferdinand of Naples had a passion
for it and commissioned Josef Haydn to compose a series of
concerti for an ensemble which was to include two *lire or-
ganizzate*. The possibilities of the instrument were extremely
limited, and the sound was considered somewhat akin to that
of the oboe so that it would not be out of place in El Moreno's
ensemble.

La Petra y la Juana also affords a glimpse of what a *maja*
would consider suitable finery for a festive occasion:

> Se puso ella aquel jubón
> .... la basquiña
> de moer con los dos flecos;
> la cofia con aquel lazo
> de varas de cintas ciento;
> la rica mantilla de
> labirinto, con el negro
> pispunte en el fistonado....[23]

The *mantilla de labirinto*, "mazy mantilla," was obviously one
worked in an elaborate pattern. The *majo* satisfies himself

---

21 Ibid., 286-87.
22 Percy A. Scholes, *The Oxford Companion to Music* (8th ed.; London,
    1950).
23 Ramón de la Cruz, *Colección*, Vol. 2, 284.

with ". . . la capa, reloj y mi juego de hebillas de plata. . . ."[24]

In the same writer's *El Petimetre* there are some specific details of the coiffure of a fashionable gentleman of the time:

> Soplado.
> Tarariri, las toallas.
> Tarariri.
> Aquí están. ¿De qué manteca?
> Soplado.
> Ninguna: trae la pomada
> de jazmines.

Soplado thereupon instructs his servant as to what suit he intends to wear and proceeds to recite a prayer under his breath, although his mind is obviously on his toilette:

> Ro, ro, ro, ro, ro; mirad
> que ayer dicen, que llevaba
> tres pelos mas en un lado,
> y un canto de real de plata
> más levantado ese bucle,
> Ro, ro, ro, ro, ro; con gracia
> este tupé, como ayer:
> bien.[25]

One of the striking manifestations of religious fervour in the eighteenth century was the processions or "pasos" in which, in graphic detail, the passion of Christ was portrayed. Apart from the scriptural aspect there was obviously the appeal to the theatrical taste of the Spanish people who delighted in the opportunity for costume display, as appears in *La presumida burlada* of Ramón de la Cruz:

> . . . si tú hubieras estado
> aquí por Semana Santa,
> y hubieras visto los Pasos,
> verias a los cabreros,
> y la gente del esparto
> vestidos de militar,
> su espadín atravesado,
> y su camisola. . . .[26]

---

24   Ibid., 285.
25   Ibid., Vol. 1, 501.
26   Ibid., 99.

Religious education, even secular education, on the other hand, was not always regarded with such enthusiasm. Ramón de la Cruz in *La comedia casera (segunda parte)* mocks the indulgence of parents who protect their child from the rigours of too much schooling:

> D. Blas.
> ¡Qué adelantada está mi hija,
> válgame, San Nicudemus!
> D. Fadrique al niño.
> ¿Mi alma, y vas á la escuela?
> Doña Elena.
> Iba; pero como el tiempo
> es tan caliente en verano
> y tan frío en el invierno,
> le he quitado hasta que tenga
> catorce años por lo menos.
> D. Fadrique.
> ¿Pero sabrá la doctrina
> cristiana?
> Doña Elena.
> No sé; yo creo
> que sí. ¿La sabes?
> Niño.
> Ya sé
> La mitad del Padre nuestro.
> D. Fadrique.
> ¡Válgame Dios qué crianza![27]

Not only education, but false religion too, is a source for satire. In *El Fandango de candil* the object for mockery is one of those worldly *abates* who thought much of the perquisites and opportunities for good living their habit provided by gaining them entrance to the houses of the wealthy where they were often entrusted with the upbringing (and sometimes corruption) of the younger members of the household:

> Abate.
> Señorito, mire usted
> qué lindo par de muchachas
> van con ese petimetre.
> Señorito.
> ¡Qué sé me dá á mí que vayan!

---

27   Ibid., 402.

A yo mío, este paseo
no me divierte, y me cansa:
vámonos hácia el Retiro
que hay flores, hácia la plaza
que hay fruta, ó á ver las calles
donde la procesion anda.
                Abate.
Hombre, esas son niñerías;
y á usted ya la edad le basta
para pensar cosas grandes,
como cortejar madamas,
conocer el vario mundo
y entrar con todos en danza.
                Señorito
¿Y si lo sabe mi madre?
                Abate.
Por ahora está ocupada
en rezar sus oraciones;
y bien sabe á quién encarga
su hijo: venga usted conmigo,
que no le daré crianza
opuesta á la de los que
mas en Madrid se señalan.
                Señorito.
Si á mí esto no me divierte.
                Abate.
Ahí vereis vuestra ignorancia:
y es menester por los mismo
que la diestra vigilancia
del ayo a quien os confian,
la venza con la enseñanza
de lo bueno y de lo malo;
porque no digais mañana
que no os enseñé de todo.[28]

To the capital from the provinces came hordes of aspirants
to employment either in the mother country or in America.
Some trusted to their native ability to secure for them the
post desired; others relied on distinction acquired through
family connections. Those from the Biscayan region or from
Galicia particularly found support in their compatriots already established. This regional nepotism is referred to by
Ramón de la Cruz in *El agente de sus negocios*:

---

28   Ibid., Vol. 2, 599.

> ... mi vecino
> dos años há que vino atravesado
> en un burro, y ya llegó al estado
> de criados, de coche y de talego,
> y eso que no es vizcaino ni gallego;
> que es decir que no debe su equipage
> al ínclito favor del paisanage.[29]

The women's liberation movement would have no cause to complain in the eighteenth century as Ramón de la Cruz makes plain in *La maja majada*:

> Alcalde.
> ¿Qué, no manda usté en su casa?
> Blas.
> Señor Alcalde, aunque sea
> descortesía: y usted
> si es casado, manda en ella?
> Alcalde.
> Sí señor, y mi muger,
> en viéndome, es la primera
> que se pone á temblar, sin
> que nadie á chistar se atreva,
> hasta que yo doy la órden.
> Blas.
> Será la señora vieja.
> Alcalde.
> No es sino moza y bonita.
> Blas.
> ¿Muchacha, bonita, y tiembla
> en entrando su marido,
> y en todo vive sujeta
> a su mercé, en este siglo?
> ¡vaya, que usté se chancea!
> ¡ningún casado es posible
> que trague esa berengena![30]

Certainly, if one is to believe that this author's playlets reflect the truth, as he avers, the disbelief of Blas is justified.

Out of such elements Ramón de la Cruz fashioned amusing tidbits to amuse the Madrid public and to leave to posterity scenes of striking realism and a faithful picture of certain classes of society in a specific period of social history.

---

29 Ibid., 200.
30 Ibid., 30.

Moratín's comedies, on the other hand, behind their lighter moments shadow a darker side of the social customs of Spanish society in the opening years of the nineteenth century. The abuse of authority with its potentially tragic consequences was obviously sufficiently common enough to induce Moratín to plead for a more understanding and enlightened attitude towards the training of the young.

A parent's or guardian's urge to manipulate those who are under his control is often inspired by motives not peculiar to time or nationality, but universal—usually the greed for gain. In *El viejo y la niña* it is the greed of her guardian that has led him to defalcation of his ward's future and thus see a suitable match for her in the septuagenarian don Roque, who guarantees not to inquire into the handling of his bride's finances. A minor point of interest in this play is a reference to the taking of snuff, so common a habit of the time:

> Don Roque.
> Vamos, Muñoz, no te enojes.
> Toma un polvo.
> Muñoz.
> ¡La zanguanga
> Del polvito! Tengo aquí.
> Don Roque.
> Arrójalo, que eso es granzas.
> Muñoz.
> Así me gusta.
> Don Roque.
> Este es
> De aquello bueno de marras,
> Del padre de la Merced.[31]

Greed is also a major factor in *El sí de las niñas*. Doña Irene sees a comfortable way of life for herself once her daughter is married to the elderly and wealthy don Diego.

The curious fact is that Moratín, the idolater of Molière, does not, as his master would have done, essay a study of the psychological aspects of the vice of greed but, more pragmatic, considers the resultant effects with a view to seeking a

---

31   Leandro Fernández de Moratín, *Obras*, Vol. 2, ed. by Aribau, *Biblioteca de Autores Españoles* (BAE) (Madrid, 1944), 341.

remedy through judicial or educational means: "Bordar, coser, leer libros devotos, oir misa, y correr por la huerta detrás de las mariposas, y echar agua en los agujeros de las hormigas."[32] A different curriculum from this, suggests Moratín, would prepare a young girl more adequately for the responsibilities of marriage and enable her to realize and cope with the problems, practical and social, of life. It is the duty of those in authority, he asserts, to maintain a personally disinterested attitude and to assure that the young are trained and guided in a way that will offer them more secure opportunities for happiness. Otherwise disaster will result. Through repressive measures, youthful initiative atrophies; fear of parental displeasure leads to hypocrisy or concealment of true feeling; and character is warped: "Esto resulta del abuso de la autoridad de la opresión que la juventud padece. . . ."[33] Jovellanos expresses views as modern and enlightened as Moratín's. In *El delincuente honrado* (1774) he has the old Spanish traditionalist Simón refer slightingly to the modern fashion of discarding the old ways for new foreign ones. Those foreign ways are of course French: ". . . no contentos con hacernos comer y vestir como la gente de extranjía, quieren tambien que estudiemos y sepamos á la francesa."[34]

In particular Simón is contemptuous of the philosophy imported from Paris which submits everything to the scrutiny of reason. Referring to a case of a man accused of killing another in a duel, he remarks scathingly:

Que vaya, que vaya ahora á defenderle tu marido con sus filosofías. Qué, ¿no hay mas que andarse matando los hombres por frioleras, y luego disculparlos con opiniones galanas? Todos estos modernos gritan: la razon, la humanidad, la naturaleza. Bueno andará el mundo cuando se haga caso de estas cosas.[35]

Jovellanos, however, soon shows that he does not share these antiquated views and, as a rebuttal, has the just and upright

32 Ibid., 420.
33 Ibid., 441.
34 Gaspar Melchor de Jovellanos, *Obras*, Vol. 46, ed. by Nocedal, *BAE* (Madrid, 1951), 85.
35 Ibid., 88-89.

Torcuato welcome the enlightenment of the new views as he meditates upon the legal methods employed at present: "¡La tortura! . . . ¡Oh nombre odioso! ¡Nombre funesto! . . . ¿Es posible que en un siglo en que se respeta la humanidad y en que la filosofía derrama su luz por todas partes, se escuchen aun entre nosotros los gritos de la inocencia oprimida?"[36]

In *Pelayo*, written in 1804 and performed for the first time in 1805, Quintana no doubt was thinking of the unhappy state of Spain under French domination, as he laments its subjugation by the Moors: "Veremundo. ¡No hay ya España, no hay patria!" The temporarily suppressed patriotic fervour of nineteenth-century Spaniards is heard in Pelayo's passionate rebuttal: "¡No hay patria, Veremundo! ¿No la lleva todo buen español dentro en su pecho?" Veremundo's excuse for his depair could be equally well applied to those who accepted French domination and sought to profit by it:

> Quien pierde a España
> no es el valor del moro; es el exceso
> de la degradación; los fuertes yacen,
> un profundo temor hiela á los buenos,
> los traidores, los débiles se venden,
> y alzan solo su frente los perversos.[37]

The parallel between the situation in the play as Pelayo wins victory and the resistance of Spain to the French is made even clearer in the closing lines: ". . . si un pueblo insolente allá algún día / al carro de su triunfo atar intenta / la nación que hoy libramos, nuestros nietos / su independencia así fuertes defiendan. . . ."[38]

The nineteenth century is well advanced before dramatists turn their attention to the society of their time. Romanticism was too much concerned with portraying idyllic or tempestuous sentiments and with seeking to paint a medieval picture full of colour and chivalry, a canvas of bright hues which

---

36   Ibid., 89.
37   Manuel José de Quintana, *Pelayo*, Vol. 5, ed. by Sainz de Robles, *El Teatro Español* (Madrid, 1943), 1062.
38   Ibid., 1108.

came not from the paint-box of history but from the feverish creations of their own imagination.

Despite such fantasy creations in this period, there are momentary contacts with reality. For example, such a moment can be seen in Larra's *No más mostrador*, in which Doña Bibiana represents the pretensions of many women of her day who wished to substitute for the confines of her husband's shop the supposed grandeur of a lady of title and fashion:

... mientras yo no tenga mi magnífica casa, y esté en un soberbio taburete recibiendo la gente del gran tono, y dando disposiciones para las arañas y los quinqués, y la mesa de juego, y las alfombras, y el ambigú, y no entren mis lacayos abriendo la mampara, y anunciando: "el conde tal ... el vizconde cual ..." y mientras no tenga palco en la ópera, y un jocquey que me acompañe al Prado por las mañanas en invierno, con mi chal en el brazo, y mi sombrilla en la mano ... me verás aburrida, morirme de tedio. ...[39]

Muérete ¡y verás!, written by Bretón de los Herreros during the first Carlist war and performed for the first time on April 27, 1837, has its plot revolving around that civil conflict and consequently betrays some of the bitterness engendered by it. Lupercio, at the very beginning of the play, watching a troop of national militiamen march by, utters this fervent wish:

> Quiera Dios
> que á los facciosos alcancen
> y los destruyan.[40]

Later Jacinta urges a suitor who seeks to quarrel with her fiancé, "Busque usted más gloria combatiendo al despotismo. ..."[41] The lament of Froilán, who is known for his predictions of disaster, may be somewhat suspect, and it contains a parody of Quintana, but there is a hint of some of the discouragement that must have been felt by many in Spain at this unhappy moment of her history:

> ¡Pobre nación!
> Volverá a gemir esclava.

39 Mariano José de Larra, *Obras completas* (Barcelona, 1886), 631.
40 Manuel Bretón de los Herreros, *Obras*, Vol. 1 (Madrid, 1883), 433.
41 Ibid., 436.

El genio del mal persigue
a la miserable España.
Tanto afán, tantos tesoros,
tanta sangre derramada,
¿de qué han servido? La hidra
de la rebelión levanta
sus cien cabezas. El cielo
nos abandona. . . . ¡No hay patria!

The patriot Pablo, although he attributes some of this gloom
to Froilán's notorious pessimism, is forced to admit:

. . . mil desastres amagan
al Estado; que peligra
la libertad.[42]

Bretón in this play also takes the opportunity of mocking
the fondness of his compatriots for the excesses of the
Romantic drama or as a wedding guest puts it: ". . . san-
deces / del siglo décimotercio."[43] Also, the romantic *coup de
théâtre* is satirized when the hero Pablo, who has been incor-
rectly reported killed on the battlefield, to confound his
faithless fiancée and his false friends, makes a startling appearance as if resurrected, dressed in an apparent shroud
and enveloped in a mysterious reddish glow.

It was Tamayo y Baus and López de Ayala who, in the
1850s, returned to a study of contemporary manners. In
such a play as *El tejado de vidrio* (1856), López de Ayala
devotes himself, though still in a somewhat humorous manner, to depicting the moral tone of the society of his day. The
Count, to preserve his reputation as a sophisticated man of
the world, is forced to give lessons in seduction to his admiring friends: "Si has de enamorarla, empieza / por no
enamorarte tú." When the neophyte Carlos happens to
exclaim "¡Ah! ¡perdona!" the Count cynically but signifi-
cantly replies,

¿Quién se atreve
en el siglo diez y nueve
a decir ese vocablo.[44]

---

42   Ibid., 437-38.
43   Ibid., 462.
44   Adelardo López de Ayala, *El tejado de vidrio* (Madrid, 1856), 12-13.

Public as well as private foibles provide the author with matter for sardonic wit—the maidservant's lover began to write "tonterías públicas" and as a result, "Le han hecho / Gobernador de provincia."[45]

Ayala's talent for comedy is overshadowed in *El tanto por ciento* (1861) by his concern about the deterioration in moral values evident in the society of his time. The characters here represent the corruption and thirst for money which had replaced the traditional codes of honour and virtue in mid-nineteenth-century Spain. Every finer quality such as friend-ship or loyalty is sacrificed to the greed of gain: "Una cosa es la amistad / y el negocio es otra cosa." Roberto, when ques-tioned concerning an unscrupulous piece of business, replies cynically:

GASPAR: ¿Qué mas ambicionas?

ROBERTO: ¿Qué mas? Sacar el negocio
           las entrañas. ¿Qué te asombra?
           Parece que tú no vives
           en este siglo.[46]

A servant betrays her master and thus excuses herself: "Y una es la lealtad, / señor, y el negocio es otra."[47] No one, according to Roberto, is immune to the power of monetary self-interest:

           Todo se da á Belcebú
           cuando media el interes
           ... Este que ves
           es el mundo.[48]

It is in his last drama, *Consuelo* (1878), however, that Ayala most clearly reveals his conviction that a miracle is needed to save Spain from complete moral bankruptcy. This is indi-cated early in the play by Fernando's phrase: "... si de esta España infelice / Dios no tiene compasión...."[49] Again in

---

45   Ibid., 33.
46   Adelardo López de Ayala, *El tanto por ciento*, Vol. 24, *Colección de autores españoles* (Leipzig, 1885), 31.
47   Ibid., 34.
48   Ibid., 99.
49   Adelardo López de Ayala, *Consuelo*, Vol. 7, ed. by Sainz de Robles, *El Teatro Español* (Madrid, 1943), 393.

scene vii it is Fernando who summarizes the prevalent mood
of the times:

> "Simple, tonto, majadero. . . ."
> Es el premio que hoy anima
> al hombre que más estima
> su conciencia que el dinero.[50]

No one, he says, is free from the influence of this "gangrena
senil." Antonia characterizes thus the decadent moral tone of
late-nineteenth-century Spanish society:

> ¿Es que de esta sociedad
> En el alma corrompida
> Ya sólo efecto produce
> La belleza que seduce
> Ó la fuerza que intimida,
> Y otras razones son vanas
> Aunque el deber las ordene?[51]

Consuelo, epitomized as the materialistic self-seeker of her
time,

> Vivirás,
> Como tantas, como tantas,
> Cercado de ostentación,
> Alma muerta, vida loca,
> Con la sonrisa en la boca
> Y el hielo en el corazón.[52]

Tamayo y Baus also was convinced of an ethical crisis in his
nation and was determined to combat it with the doctrine of
Christian love and charity. In the prologue to one of his first
works, *Ángela* (1852), he avows the purpose of using his
dramatic writings as didactic vehicles to set moral examples:

En el estado en que la sociedad se encuentra es preciso llamarla al
camino de la regeneración, despertando en ella el germen de los
sentimientos generosos; es indispensable luchar con el egoísmo
para vencerlo con el eficaz auxilio de la compasión, virtud la más
noble y santa de la virtudes.[53]

---

50 Ibid., 398.
51 Ibid., 478.
52 Ibid., 484.
53 Manuel Tamayo y Baus, *Obras*, Vol. 1, ed. by Pidal y Mon (Madrid, 1898), 193-94.

The lessons appear: the theme of the pursuit of wealth, the dominant passion of the time, is shown to threaten other nobler motives in such a play as *Lo positivo* (1862). As one of the characters put it: "En el siglo en que vivimos, todo el mundo ha dado en creer que la felicidad es cosa que se compra con el dinero." In *Lances de honor* (1863) he condemns the pernicious but still not uncommon practice of resorting to the duel as a means of solving actual or imagined slights to the touchy, traditional code of honour.

The incongruous element in this over-used attempt of mid-century writers to concern themselves with contemporary mores and vices in order to extirpate them and so lead their country back to a more worthy and moral path is that the expression of ideas is so full of the previous age's rhetoric and that the sentimental sobs or melodramatic situations come perilously close to undermining the sincerity of the message.

It will be left to writers like Pérez Galdós or Benavente, whose dramatic work may by initiated in the nineteenth century but whose finest achievements belong technically to the twentieth, to formulate a type of drama that actually represents the society in which they lived and who, for the most part, possess the art of making their characters sound of the actual period.

FOUR

TWENTIETH-CENTURY SPANISH DRAMA: IN DEFENSE OF LIBERTY

A. A. Borrás
Wilfrid Laurier University

Theatre is the most immediate of the arts; it speaks directly, making an effect instantly and spontaneously, or not at all. In addition, no preparation is required for the theatre: the groundling and the intellectual will each find different things therein.[1] Its primeval status in literary history proves that it has been an instrument for the expression of man's soul since the very beginning. Spain's early Middle Ages plays of mockery, which were crude and farcical parodies of things ecclesiastical, marked the beginning of the short, one-act play which has survived through to modern times. This seed of rebellion against established

---

1 George E. Wellwarth, *Underground Spanish Theatre* (University Park: Pennsylvania State University Press, 1972), 2.

order is vibrant in twentieth-century Spanish drama, even
though a civil war and paralyzing censorship rules have
caused some of the best Spanish plays to be written and
staged in countries other than Spain: Mexico, Argentina,
and Puerto Rico. This essay contains a brief outline of the
main playwrights of Spanish contemporary theatre and
examines, in some detail, a representative play from each of
three exile dramatists.

The father of twentieth-century Spanish theatre is Jacinto
Benavente (1866-1954), born in Madrid, the son of a famous
pediatrician. He spoke French, English, and Italian and
knew the works of the great playwrights of his time (Wilde,
Maeterlinck, D'Annunzio, Ibsen, Shaw). The essential element in Benavente's dramatic formula is a subtle irony used
to criticize various components of society, mainly the aristoc-
racy and the upper middle class. His satire is sharp but not
corrosive, and while his scepticism shows a mistrust of society, Benavente believes in love as a most ennobling sentiment. His plays present a mixture of idealism and satire
clothed in elegant dialogue.

Benavente reacted against the prevailing grandiloquent,
melodramatic plays of the nineteenth century, best charac-
terized by those of Echegaray. He delighted audiences with
numerous presentations of the everyday happenings of the
common man, his 172 plays falling into two basic categories,
the psychological and the satirical.[2] Two stand out from all
the rest: *Los intereses creados* (*Vested Interests*, 1907) and *La
Malquerida* (*The Passion Flower*, 1913). In *Los intereses creados*, a
comedy of intrigue, he uses the characters from the *Com-
media dell'arte* and shows how men are easily corrupted, and
like puppets are moved by the hidden threads of good and
evil passions. Leandro and Crispín, master and servant who
symbolize good and evil, serve to show that in spite of egoism
and materialistic ambitions there exists true, indestructible,
pure love. *La Malquerida* is a forceful play based on the
Hippolytus-Phaedra theme; Esteban's love for his step-

---

2   Marcelino C. Peñuelas, *Jacinto Benavente*, trans. by Kay Engler (New
    York: Twayne Publishers, 1968), 68.

daughter, Acacia, is evident, but Acacia's love for her step-father remains concealed almost until the end of the play. Esteban had hired a man to murder Acacia's fiance, and when attempting to escape justice he kills Raimunda, Acacia's mother. Acacia is therefore saved from her love as she refuses to follow her mother's murderer. Benavente's psychological penetration of the female character seen here is characteristic of his theatre.

When Benavente won the Nobel Prize for Literature in 1922 he had already entered the less remarkable period of his career (1920-1954). One of his later dramas, *Abdicación* (*Abdication*, 1948), is noteworthy, nevertheless, for its por-trayal of Old Spain in contrast with the modern age. He was both a realist and an idealist, and therefore his satire lacks the will to reform the society that it ridicules. Benavente's weak-ness lies in the fact that his theatrical formula remained essentially unchanged, despite the fact that between his first and his last play the world had experienced two major wars, and Spain a civil war.

The year 1936 marks not only the beginning of the Spanish Civil War, but also the loss of two great dramatists: the murder of Federico García Lorca and the death of Ramón del Valle-Inclán. Quite probably, Lorca's was the finest poetic theatre to be had since that of the Golden Age, the treasures of which he took to the provinces when he directed the *Teatro Universitario*. This touring company, along with a second one, was set up under the auspices of the Ministry of Culture and Public Information founded in 1931 by the Spanish Republic.

Ramón del Valle-Inclán draws inspirational material from the folklore of his native region, elevating it to a universal plane as does Lorca. He is the most original dramatist of the twentieth century in the sense that the changes he made in drama over the Naturalist mode were truly prophetic. The intrinsic development of his theatre reveals a continual for-mal and thematic renovation, setting it apart from other dramatic tendencies of the period.

Valle-Inclán's masterpiece is *Divinas palabras* (*Divine Words*, 1913), premiered in 1933. The protagonist could be

considered to be Galicia, its rural setting imbued with super-
stition, mystery, and folklore. A key figure in the play is the
hydrocephalic idiot, who, by virtue of being a touchstone,
gives cohesion to the twenty scenes in the drama. Through
the idiot, Valle-Inclán can express the themes of avarice,
original sin, innocence, cruelty, and the desperation of humanity. Included in the play also are the themes of death,
incest, promiscuity, lust, and lack of meaning in life, all
represented in the absurd, materialistic struggle for existence.

Valle-Inclán does not offer solutions to social, political, or
moral problems. Rather, he presents them through abnormal characters (since the others dare not express them) who
often have a catalytic function in the drama, provoking
others to act. Indeed, it is in the mythical, the absurd, and the
abnormal characters that this playwright's message is to be
found.

Valle-Inclán's theatre reflects an increasingly negative
view of the world, so that he comes to look down on his
characters whom he considers inferior to himself. This attitude is expressed in the stage of his *esperpento*, an esthetic
invented by Goya, in which classic heroes are deformed and
Spain is seen as a grotesque deformation of European civilization. It is in his *esperpento Los cuernos de don Friolera* (*The
Horns of Don Friolera*, 1921) that a clear attack against the
Calderonian honour theme is found, the latter being compared to the cruelty and dogmatism found in the Bible.

García Lorca's theatre is a perfect fusion of music, art, and
poetry. His formula, both simple and complex, reveals the
central theme of honour. Characters fight to preserve their
name, tradition, and moral laws, but the maintenance of the
status quo sets off a series of chain reactions which lead to
frustration of love, despair, and death. Other themes are
present: separation-alienation; reality versus desire; social,
political, and moral problems; the confrontation of two vital,
uncompromising forces, authority and liberty. Regardless of
the perspective taken, the vehicle of expression is constant in
the use of unique imagery and symbols such as horses, bulls,
blood, knives, the earth, moon, and rivers. Lorca's ability to

interpret popular traditions and folkways evident throughout his works enhances their exotic qualities.

Federico García Lorca's theatre progressed gradually toward an essentially human one, so that one may observe a statement made in 1933, "I believe sincerely that theatre is not nor can not be anything else but emotion and poetry in word, action and gestures,"[3] in contrast with a judgment made by Lorca three years later, and only months before his death, "In these times of drama, the artist ought to laugh and cry with his public. You have to forget the lilies and get up to your waist in mud to help those that are looking for lilies. As for myself, I have a real desire to communicate with others. For this reason I have knocked at the doors of theatre and it is to theatre that I devote all my sensitivity."[4]

Lorca's last drama, *La casa de Bernarda Alba* (*Bernarda Alba's House*, 1936), forms the trilogy of tragic love together with *Bodas de sangre* (*Blood Wedding*) and *Yerma*. The protagonist is Bernarda, a tyrannical, authoritative, fanatical mother who supresses all feelings of love and desire in her daughters. The atmosphere of sterility is depicted by the white walls. Bernarda's daughters are forced to live isolated in a suffocating atmosphere where all passions are suppressed in order to preserve the honour code. Conflict arises from the opposed forces of Bernarda's authority and power and the daughters' quest for freedom. There is no dialogue, no compromise. The end result is spiritual death for all and Adela's suicide.

No doubt, in the political interpretation of the drama, Bernarda represents narrow, traditional, intolerant Spain, in short, repression in that country or any other country. It is worth noting that the play was not staged in Spain until 1964, some twenty-eight years after it was written!

The year 1936 not only marked Lorca's last drama and the beginning of the Spanish Civil War, but heralded a new era in European literature. In the novel and poetry this new

---

3 Federico García Lorca, *Obras completas* (5th ed.; Madrid: Aguilar, 1963), 1739. The translation into English is mine, as are all others in this essay.

4 Ibid., 1814.

spirit meant the abandonment of dehumanization of art and
the taking on of what has been called by the Spanish critic,
Ignacio Soldevila Durante, "the awareness of human compromise." Unfortunately, the Spanish drama did not de-
velop as other genres, for with a few exceptions, most
dramatists relied on well-worn themes, situations, and
forms. Established dramatists of the thirties, such as Enrique
Jardiel Poncela, Miguel Mihura, López Rubio, and Ruiz
Iriarte, continued to write escapist literature, *teatro de evasión*,
the purpose of which was to entertain rather than to appeal
to man's conscience.

It must be pointed out that in the trajectory of the Spanish
drama there is a gap between the poetic theatre of García
Lorca and Casona of the thirties and forties and Buero
Vallejo's and Alfonso Sastre's realistic, social theatre of the
forties and fifties. The theatre of the Spanish exile ligatures
these two esthetics.

The exile theatre of Rafael Alberti, Pedro Salinas, and
Max Aub[5] is a continuation of the rich Spanish tradition of
Valle-Inclán and Lorca, the evolution of which was truncated
with the coming of the Civil War and the severe censorship
which ensued. One of the most significant functions of this
exile theatre is that it maintained a historical continuity of
Spain's theatre. It was Domingo Pérez Minik who observed
that Spanish exiles stand out from all other exiles of all ages,
be they from the French Revolution, the Imperial Counter-
revolution or Russian émigrés from various political stages;
Spanish exiles do not show a change of mentality, sensibility,
or beliefs because of the impact of foreign cultures, but,
rather, delve deeper into their own soul.[6]

The condition of exile puts a peculiar psychological strain
on writers which, ironically, for Spanish intellectuals only
serves to nourish their creative introspection into the meaning of Spanish history and society. The relationship of life,

---

5 Each spent his exile in a different country: Alberti (1902-) went to
   Argentina; Salinas (1891-1951) to the U.S.; Aub (1903-1972) to
   Mexico.
6 Domingo Pérez Minik, *Teatro europeo contemporáneo* (Madrid:
   Ediciones Guadarrama, 1961), 494.

literature, and history appears closer than ever in their literature, which will become evident in the discussion of various
dramas of Alberti, Salinas, and Aub.

When Rafael Alberti was fifteen he had already decided
upon painting as a vocation, having already painted the
ships, beaches, waves, salt marshes, trees, and castles of his
beloved Bay of Cádiz, a place which never left his heart. His
literary bent revealed itself later, at age twenty-two, when he
wrote his first book of poems, *Marinero en tierra (Land Seaman)*
for which he received the National Prize for Literature.
Painting and poetry greatly influenced Alberti's dramatic
production, and the play in which startling imagery, plasticity, music, and rhythm find their most striking synthesis is his
masterpiece, *Noche de guerra en el Museo del Prado* (*A Night of
War in the Prado Museum*, 1956).

Alberti's handling of the historical substratum in *A Night of
War in the Prado Museum* is unique in Spanish drama. It was
common starting in the 1950s for Spain's social dramatists to
use historical distancing while addressing themselves to current political and social problems in order not to clash with
the censors, but Alberti's superimposition of the 1808 upris-
ing against Napoleonic forces on the popular resistance in
the Spanish Civil War must be considered ingenious. Ruiz
Ramón has remarked on Alberti's dramatic handling of
these two epochs in the following way:

Alberti, with great originality and efficacy, makes the technique of
distancing *function* as a technique of identification. The heroism of
the people, their spontaneity for unifying and resisting, their capacity for insolence and for charm, their consciousness of the cause
as a popular cause, their reaction to injustice and treason of which
they are victims, the horrors and cruelty of war, the symbolic
execution of the culprits reflect at the same time, two nights of war,
integrated in dramatic unity, and identified in form and content,
two nights separated by time—1808, 1936—but uniform in meaning.[7]

In the prologue, the author Alberti addresses his audience
from the stage, the central room of the Prado Museum, the

7   Ruiz Ramón, *Historia del teatro español: Siglo XX* (Madrid: Alianza
Editorial, 1971), 236.

background of which is a movie screen. Museum paintings
will be projected from this screen; characters from Goya and
Velázquez and other painters, in all their vibrant energy and
expressive realism, will become the characters of the drama.
Madrid is being bombed and the great Spanish treasures, in
danger of being destroyed, must be removed to the basement. (The author then reminisces about his inspirational
visits to the Prado as a young man.) What follows is a pictorial
procession of Spanish history represented by paintings of
Goya, Rubens, Velázquez, Titian, and others. The only "real"
characters are two militiamen who comment on the bombing
activities over Madrid, and thus make the time transition to
1936. But the two historical events are also integrated
through the dialogue of the personages portrayed in the art
works. In an ingenious fashion, Alberti lets them speak, so
that in and by their human potentiality they articulate the
organic realities of war and their instinctive response to
them:

MANCO (Maimed One):   What other arms did we have the 2nd of
                      May? Let's see, Grinder! You have a rifle.
                      Give your knife to the student.

ESTUDIANTE (The Student):   (Taking the knife.) But now it's dif-
                            ferent. Those cannons that are
                            shooting must be something new.

MANCO: That's the way it goes. We are people of the street, people
         used to fighting without arms. We won't need arms.
         They are hidden everywhere. And if they're no good,
         we'll use our nails and our teeth! Any shirtcollar fighter
         will soon find out![8]

The heroism of the people is, without doubt, the unifying
theme of the drama, thus the manner in which Alberti
achieves this quality in his characters deserves attention. The
fact that the author extracts them (with the exception of the
two militiamen) primarily from paintings, sketches, and
etchings of Goya is quite significant. Goya invented the *esper-*
pento, his classic heroes deformed, as is their image in a

---

8   Rafael Alberti, *Noche de guerra en el Museo del Prado* (Buenos Aires:
    Ediciones Losange, 1956), 48-49.

concave or convex mirror. By his individualistic genius, he restored the realist tradition in Spanish art, reacting against the sentimental idealization of official painting. As if it were not enough that he chose Goya's artistic interpretations of humanity to achieve heroism in his characters, he has them *reinterpret* their condition in the context of the pictures in which they occur. This heightening of human pathos is evident in the following dialogue which takes place while the group is making a barricade with sandbags, against Napoleon:

MANCO: ... You don't seem to have much pep, do you? What's your name?

FUSILADO   (The One Who Has Been Shot): (Shrugging his shoulders.) Me? Pshaw! Me they shot in Moncloa. With my hands tied. On the 2nd of May at the Puerta del Sol. Those wicked French! I don't know what my name is. I've forgotten it. You can call me Fusilado.

MANCO: (Picking up the leather winebag and giving it to him.) Take this. (While he is drinking.) And what were you?

FUSILADO: A muleteer. Between Toledo and Madrid. I arrived the night before.... (After a brief pause.) Well, I feel better now. (To the grinder.) Let's go.

AMOLADOR (The grinder):   (He tries to walk, but falls on his knees.) Take this knife out of my bones. I can hardly breathe.

MANCO: (Trying to take the knife out of him, but it is embedded in his chest right up to the hilt.) Let's see! (To Fusilado.) How about you helping. It's too deep for one hand alone.

FUSILADO: (Managing to get it out.) That was an awful thing. Why did they do it?

AMOLADOR: For a knife. I was a grinder. I sharpened knives in the street.... They found one I had buried in a pot of geraniums. They hanged me.... Then they stuck it in me ... and they left (p. 21).

The heroism of the people is also brought out by qualitative judgments made on them such as "The people never die, it is said, and it is true," or "The people have a good sense of smell, they have snouts like dogs. They know that they are being deceived and nothing more. They understand little

about discourses." However, the indomitable spirit of the
people is usually brought out in grotesque images, such as
that of the *Descabezado* (The Beheaded One). He comes out
on stage clamouring for justice, and even if they have cut off
his head with an ax, it will go on talking until the end of the
world, he affirms. In keeping with the "esperpentic" mold in
which the drama is conceived, Alberti creates a horrendous
scene in which the *Descabezado*, in response to the thunder-
ous discharge of firearms, jumps to the defense of Madrid,
seizing his severed head by the hairs, and thrusts it through
the museum door as a mighty weapon with a "hundred
thousand rays of hate inside it." As his body falls lifeless to the
ground, the consensus is that he is not dead because he
cannot die, just as none of the people dies.

"Esperpentic" images such as these abound in the drama.
Velázquez's portrait of Philip iv's favourite jester, D. Sebas-
tián de Morra, for example, is used by Alberti to reveal the
disgraced state of this monarch and the distasteful legacy he
left to Spanish history. When we view the horrific dimensions of such characters who represent the enemies of
people's freedom, grotesque portraits such as that of
Godoy—seen as a fat, spongy frog with saliva dripping onto
his belly—we wonder in amazement at the spontaneous regeneration of those people whom the artists made eternal on
their canvases. And of course we marvel at the dramatist's
ability to show, through the medium of art, the political
relevance of Spain's historical figures, and the role they
played in determining her history. The success of the play, as
a political play, derives from the fact that the political aspect
flows naturally from the drama felt within the Spanish soul.
Alberti's artistic sensitivity no doubt must have influenced
the quality of the play. Ortega y Gasset was known to have
said that Velázquez's paintings gave him a strange feeling, as
if he were not looking at the portraits, but, rather, that the
portraits were looking at him. With Alberti, they must not
only have looked at him, but they surely told him many
secrets also.

Pedro Salinas lived with Spain in the back of his mind, or
rather, with Spain on his shoulders, a burden both sweet and

heavy. In his dramas he sets forth to remove the masks and disguises which conceal truth from our eyes, but not to right wrongs or find solutions to problems. His compulsion was to discover life, and, if his theatre has any message, it is to enjoy life, to taste it both happily and painfully. His satirical plays, full of irony and poetry, express the same vision of the world: a defense of human life, always concrete, against any attempt of alienation or exploitation.

The best of these satirical plays, indeed, Salinas's masterpiece, is *Los santos* (*The Saints*). And it is not without irony that the only drama *not* published in Spain is precisely his masterpiece.[9] One wonders if Pérez Minik took this play into consideration when he wrote: "It fills us with emotion to perceive that in none of his stage creations does there arise any protest born of that condition of exile which was his lot to live."[10] It is true that most of Salinas's plays lack a Spanish ambience, portraying, rather, universal characters beset by human failures, misfortunes, and disillusionment, but there are three dramas that are set solidly in a Spanish atmosphere: *La fuente del arcángel* (*Fountain of the Archangel*), *La estratosfera* (*The Stratosphere*), and *Los santos*, with his most skillful handling of the Spanish political theme being found in the latter play. Five characters, prisoners held by a Falangist lieutenant, sergeant, and soldiers, are locked in the basement of a collegiate church in the town of Vivanca, in New Castile, to await death as punishment for their crimes. (One might note the nature of some of the crimes: that of a mother who protested the killing of her pacifist son; desertion on the part of an elderly man who refused to build a gallows from which to hang prisoners.)

The brutal reality of this civil war vignette is moderated by the presence of the supernatural as Salinas integrates saints with people in order to bring about a solution to the prisoners' predicament. This technique is almost always used in Salinas's work; according to Ruiz Ramón, there is usually an "intervention of supernatural forces to resolve a planted

---

9 *Los santos* was published posthumously in *Cuadernos Americanos* 13/3 (1954), 265-91.
10 Domingo Pérez Minik, *Teatro europeo*, 506.

situation to show the presence of protective gods in human existence."[11] No doubt, such a formula bespeaks a certain idealism on the part of the author, a courageous will to save the world.

The five prisoners reflect the total spectrum of civil war atmosphere and suffering: problems of mistaken identity, treason, repression, suspicion, pacifism, tyranny, brutal killings. Salinas's protest of civil war conditions cannot be considered to be veiled, as the following dialogue (and it is worth noting that in his works the dialogue, not the action, is the source of dramatic tension) between the grieving mother, a prostitute, and a Republican sergeant reveals:

MADRE: For nothing, child . . . they killed him on me for nothing . . . they'll kill you for nothing . . . everyone, they're killing us all for nothing . . . saying things quickly and no one understanding them. . . . For no reason.

PALMITO: Maybe you're right . . . It's that some people are born to kill and others are born to be killed. . . . That's the way the law must be. . . .

OROZCO: No, that's not the law, it's the opposite, it's injustice, it's tyranny, it's . . . (p. 284).

In spite of vivid protests such as these, *Los santos* reveals a radical humanism, an urge on the part of its author to show that all human needs are the same. One of the prisoners, a nun, although wrongly accused, chooses not to prove her innocence: "Do you not see that if I saved myself, if they pardoned me, on top of being punished, poor things, they would be envious. They would die jealous, envying me, hating me. This way we will die, all of us loving one another, pitying one another. Those who didn't feel like brothers in life still can die like brothers" (p. 289). To die for the cause of brotherhood is a pathetic and paradoxical commentary on Spain's Civil War; to give one's life for an absolute is an authentic expression of the Spanish character.

Typical of Salinas's esthetic is the use of a commonplace idea or object to infer a greater spiritual truth, this being, perhaps, the hallmark of a poet. In this play he makes use of

11   Ruiz Ramón, *Historia*, 284.

a very prosaic object as a touchstone to illustrate that man's basic needs are the same—the cigarette. The observation is made that in general, humanity is stingy, but in the case of tobacco and smoking, people tend to be generous. The proof is that the Falangists threw, from their trenches, packs of cigarettes to the Republican sergeant. The cigarette becomes in the play a sign of common suffering and understanding.

Another way in which Salinas shows his desire to redeem humanity is his humane treatment of the prostitute, Palmito, whose worldliness forms a stark contrast to the naïvete of the other prisoners. For example, the elderly pacifist, Severio, asks her outright what her profession is, and the quiet-mannered youth, Paulino, guilelessly tells her that her evilness is not very apparent. The final image we have of Palmito is one in which she is kneeling before the mother, her head in her lap, where she is lulled to sleep. Salinas makes no judgments on her virtue; she is merely part of humanity, condemned to die for a crime she did not commit.

The intercession of the saints and their role in saving the lives of the prisoners is the most surprising element in the play, even though the statues' presence is apparent from the very beginning. They startle and instill fear and even mistrust in those who see them, so that when they become ambulatory and take on the appearance of the prisoners, we are surprised, but not shocked.

Many interpretations of this transfiguration of reality might be proffered. Did Salinas intend to point to the ironical consequences of war? The attacks on churches and the clergy and subsequent counterattacks that occurred during the Civil War belong to history, but as in all war situations, sometimes victims fall at the hand of their own side, out of confusion and misunderstanding; here the irony is that the saints brought salvation to the Republicans held captive by the Falangists. Or did Salinas envision that history would absolve the exiles, those who lost the war, in the same way that the saints intervened to save the condemned?

Pedro Salinas was one of the finest poets that Spain ever produced, and therefore, in characterizing his theatre, one cannot help but appreciate its poetic qualities. His is not

evasive like Casona's, steeped in mystery and phantas-
magoria, nor is it given to the modern existential debate, but,
rather, it is based squarely on life in all its simple and profound revelations. Pérez Minik believes that Salinas's theatre
belongs to tomorrow, the rightful place for this exiled
dramatist of vision.

Max Aub spent thirty years, from 1942 to 1972, in Mexico,
bearing witness to the human suffering that he saw and
experienced. His theatre of exile shows one constant preoccupation: the responsibility of man for his fellow man. The
Spanish Civil War and its myriad consequences, the horrors
of World War ii, the Cold War, the Korean conflict, the
Cuban Revolution, and, of course, the circumstances of his
own exile, inculcated in Aub the profound conviction to
denounce the lamentable socio-political conditions of man.
This consciousness of man's moral responsibility to man,
which inspires Aub to write, is precisely the esthetic emotion
which he attempts to incarnate in his characters and evoke in
his audience.

The Spanish Civil War, the true matrix of his thematic
material, has given to Aub's dramas many existentialist types
such as the rebel, the prisoner, the political refugee, and the
exile, whose confinement in space and in time produces a
profound spiritual oppression. They are condemned to live
an ineffectual existence, and although they may gain physical freedom, they cannot replenish the spiritual void which
has grown inside them during their period of imprisonment
or banishment.

In Aub's last two dramas, written in 1968, *El cerco* (*The
Siege*) and *Retrato de un general* (*Portrait of a General*),[12] he
treats the themes of Ché Guevara's revolution in Bolivia and
the Vietnam War, political themes well worn in the conscience of modern society. For Aub there was nothing worse
than indifference to the unjust suffering of one's fellow
man. The author makes it clear that it is not important
whether Ché's ideals were right or wrong; what is significant
is that he was a man of courage committed to a cause which

---

12   Max Aub, *El cerco* (México: Joaquín Mortiz, 1968); Aub, *Retrato de un
     general* (México: Joaquín Mortiz, 1969).

he believed proper and for which he was willing to die. Pertinent details from Guevara's diary serve as a basis for the dialogue which is mainly in the form of debate. Aub recreates the last days of Ché's campaign in the Bolivian mountains when his efforts to foment a successful revolution were thwarted by the impossible circumstances surrounding him. The drama is not one of action, but reflection, and while it tells of one man's hopes, it breathes futility. At the same time, the setting of the savage mountains, the strange tongues of primitive people, and the dauntless courage of a handful of sick and hungry men give the play a romantic quality.

With *Portrait of a General* Aub has wittingly made a sacrifice: he has flouted the definition of drama, and because of the form this work takes, he knows that it will not be staged. In the preface he writes:

Getting back to theatre, what did I not do for it? I served it in a million ways. Now it is time for the roles to be changed and have it serve me: not be at its disposal, but rather it be at my disposal: let it lend me its means which, after all, are the ones that I have handled most easily since a child. Instead of writing articles or essays, I put together scenes. When I proposed to have my works performed, I was not successful. Now, it is all the same to me, I have no objections. Maybe my readers will; I am sorry. It is my fault, I accept it, and I take a deep bow, stretching out my arm to the side, even though it might be hard for me to straighten up.

All this naturally does not resolve if what follows is theatre or not, even leaving aside, that for me, there is no drama or comedy comparable to (those in) the newspaper columns if a person sits down to read them as if they were before a stage.

It is with this independent stance that Aub wrote *Portrait of a General* in 1968, when newspapers, radio, and television were satiating the public with news about the Vietnam War. One might ask why he would choose such an overwrought theme. The probable reason is that he, as an exile from Spain's Civil War, and thus sensitized to the debatable justification and horrifying realities of the Indochina conflict, saw in it the opportunity to give free reign to his political ideas. The Spanish critic, José Monleón, describes Aub's usage of this wartime prop: "The dialogue takes place this time during the Vietnam War, but it is obvious . . . that that is the backdrop for a new and updated re-encounter of Aub with all his political phantoms of the past."[13]

Monleón's use of the word "phantom" is very appropriate, for indeed the political debates regarding communism versus capitalism serve only to confound and haunt the conscience of the general.

Portrait of a General is a static drama in which an American general finds himself face to face with a Vietnamese prisoner, a companion of his thirty years earlier in the International Brigades in the Spanish Civil War. After a series of ideological debates between the two veterans, and later with the general's son, the prisoner is shot by the general. It is interesting as a psychological drama of exile: one feels keenly the gradual rending of the general's soul. The strain which is felt in and through the general is one that is very well known to an exile.

The play, or dramatic essay, as Francisco Ruiz Ramón considers it, is essentially a monologue, for the general's wife and son and the prisoner are merely various facets of the general's reality. And the fact that the general and the prisoner are veterans of Spain's Civil War where they fought Fascism, and now are adversaries in the Vietnam War, is significant; it establishes the protean nature of political convictions. The plasticity of the dialogue is such that the debate of the general and the prisoner, who are outwardly opposed, is not so much one of protagonist versus antagonist, but of two individuals, each one trying to maintain his integrity in the face of the other. Aub does not set out to contrast qualitatively capitalism and communism, for to do so would be pointless and propagandistic. He adopts neither, but rather would prefer to see a humanist-socialist political system.

The general is a tragic figure. He kills the prisoner after he can no longer bear his taunting remarks, his jibes, his ridiculing laughter. He has reviewed the past thirty years of his military career and regards himself a failure. He hears the prisoner say, "We are weaker than you but we will win,"

---

13   José Monleón, *El teatro de Max Aub* (Madrid: Ediciones Taurus, 1971), 132.

"What is your justification for being here, to show that you are the most powerful, which you are?" and "What about all the torture and cruelty that is usually associated only with savages and fanatics?" These are the harsh truths that drive the general insane.

The technique by which Aub presents the political theme and carries out the psychological development of the protagonist is interesting. We have already said that the drama is a monologue, with speeches being doled out by the general to his wife, son, prisoner, and adjutant. But I think that the drama, which takes place in the mind of the general, is also a dream. This is proven by the fact that the general appears to have no recollection of having seen his son, who has engaged in lengthy dialogue with him, the prisoner, and his wife. It is curious that the dialogue that takes place in the last scene is identical to one in the opening scenes; in other words the prisoner is introduced into the early part of the drama with the same words with which the son is introduced formally. (Prior to this formal introduction, he had "slipped in," as the stage directions read, in the latter half, to play the role of the young anarchist.) The son is brought in by the adjutant just after the prisoner has been shot, and just as in a nightmare, when the emotional climax has been reached, the dream starts over again, with the action repeating itself and roles being fluid. This time it is the general's confrontation with his son that disturbs him. "The one who hasn't changed is you" says the son, whereupon, the general starts to howl, uncontrollably, like a dog in the night, as the curtain falls. (The howling of dogs had always caused a phobic reaction in the general.) Furthermore, what more appropriate mode of communication could one expect for an exile than a dream? Dreams are the only medium of action for those forbidden to act according to their will, for those who lack freedom.

When reading Max Aub's postwar dramas, we never lose sight of his exiled position, his uncompromising attitude of protest. Of exile, Aub has said:

[It] is a natural condition for every writer because there is always a spiritual distance between him and others which makes him exiled in his own country. Authors the world over who have any impor-

tant work have been at one time or another in jail. . . . Only the
great lyric poets are free from it because their exile is interior: they
live removed from people, they live within themselves.[14]

That he continued to write prolifically with ferocious dedication, hoping and waiting for his dramas to be performed and
appreciated, is remarkable.[15]

Let us now pick up the thread of the drama in Spain.
When the Spanish Civil War broke out, Antonio Buero Vallejo, a major dramatist of the twentieth century, was twenty
years old. He left school and served in the Republican
medical corps for three years. Buero was in Valencia, one of
the last Republican strongholds, when the legitimate gov-
ernment was overthrown by Franco's forces. Unable to get a
train out of Valencia, he was arrested and taken to the bull
ring, where hundreds like himself were destined for concen-
tration camps. He was sentenced to life imprisonment but
was released on parole in 1946. In 1949 Buero won the
coveted Lope de Vega Prize for the best unperformed play
for his *Historia de una escalera (Story of a Stairway)*.

Historia de una escalera was a great success and had a profound impact on Spanish theatre. The play has its central
focus on a grimy, dark stairway that leads to the apartments
of three generations of a family that knows only disillusionment, disappointment, and death. The plight of Madrid's
immobile middle class is captured.

Government-imposed censorship (since 1939) provided
for dismissing all works deemed offensive to the very conser-
vative political and moral order of the ruling establishment.
This meant that most theatre in the first decade after the war
comprized either escapist comedies or propagandistic plays
urging a return to traditional values upheld by the new gov-
ernment. After 1949, Buero had nineteen of the plays per-

14   Max Aub, *Diario de Barcelona* (25 de julio, 1972), 20.
15   For a more detailed study of the psychology of the exile see my
     articles, "The Ideology of the Spanish Exile Max Aub," *The Theatre
     Annual* (December, 1969), 80-90; and "Exiles in the Theatre of Max
     Aub," *The Theatre Annual* (December, 1973), 19-27. For a broad
     study on Max Aub, see the books of José Monleón, Ignacio Sol-
     devila, and A. A. Borrás.

formed in Spain, skillfully managing to manoeuvre around censorship hurdles. While *Historia de una escalera* was a cornerstone for the modern Spanish drama, his *El tragaluz* (*The Basement Window*), performed almost twenty years later in 1967, is of equal significance, as it was the first Spanish play to portray sympathetically the tragic circumstances of those who had lost the war.[16] Keeping within the confines of censorship, this play does not expose the nerve of civil war suffering by direct reference to the conflict, but rather it alludes to the tragedy of a divided people through the analogy of family discord and the suggestion of psychological destruction and demoralization.[17] Most of Buero's works portray the poor and the humble in their anguished world of frustration and spiritual dissatisfaction, but although they appear outwardly defeated by their circumstances, many achieve an internal victory by their refusal to compromise. Buero's concept of tragedy is a positive one which proposes an encounter with the truth which may free man from his spiritual blindness.[18]

Buero Vallejo shared the desire to see the postwar Spanish theatre freed from the restrictions of form and expression with another fine social dramatist, Alfonso Sastre, born in 1926. What they disagreed on, however, was the degree to which innovations in content and form should be carried out. Sastre argued that Buero was too conformist, making too many concessions. Buero, on the other hand, accused Sastre of writing theatre which was impossible to be staged in Spain.[19]

Sastre belonged to a group known as *Teatro de Agitación Social* which understood that dramatic intention could be in the form of agitation or propaganda according to the religious or political tastes of the dramatist. Theatre was not for

---

16 Antonio Buero Vallejo, *El tragaluz: experimento en dos partes*, ed. by Anthony M. Pasquariello and Patricia W. O'Connor (New York: Charles Scribner's Sons, 1977), 7.

17 Ibid., 9.

18 Martha T. Halsey, *Antonio Buero Vallejo* (New York: Twayne Publishers, 1973), 150.

19 Anthony M. Pasquariello, "Alfonso Sastre y 'Escuadra hacia la muerte,'" *Hispanófila* 15 (Mayo, 1962), 57-63.

the purpose of pleasure; rather, it was to awaken the people to the social, ethical, and political problems of the time. Sastre saw theatre as *arte de urgencia* which should deal with the vital themes of salvation, repentance, culpability, responsibility, and liberty.

Sastre's masterpiece, *Escuadra hacia la muerte* (*Death Squad*, 1953) contains all those ingredients of social theatre defined by the author. A squad of five soldiers and their leader, all being punished for various crimes, is charged with awaiting the enemy offensive during an imaginary World War III. All are defeated human beings: keenly aware of their culpability, they are looking for a way to salvation. The first act ends with the brutal killing of their leader, inflicted collectively by the entire squad, as the youngest, Luis, stands guard. After the initial jubilation over the elimination of their tyrannical leader subsides, feelings of recrimination and doubt set in. The group disintegrates; some desert; one commits suicide; one surrenders to the enemy; and Pedro accepts punishment by waiting for the military authorities. In the face of this agonizing reality, Luis asks "Why?" To the questions of life and the universe there are no answers, for, as Pedro replies, "El único que podía hablar está callado." (The only one who could talk is quiet.)

It is unfortunate that a dramatist so talented has been deprived of a normal communication with the public which would have proved mutually beneficial. Sastre's theatre, seen by some critics as overly intellectual and espousing revolutionary philosophies, has been condemned to be a solitary act.

Since the beginning of the 1960s, or perhaps earlier, there has developed in Spain a flourishing "underground" theatre of high quality, in spite of a vigilant censorship. Regardless of varied style, form, and results, this theatre is one of negation and denunciation, as Buero's and Sastre's before it. Due to difficulties of publication and production, however, it lacks the social audience so necessary as its critical conscience and esthetic sounding board; authors have been denied the benefit of seeing their works under performance conditions.[20]

---

20 Space does not permit the treatment of such fine dramatists as José

Two of Spain's contemporary dramatists who have had an opportunity to publish and produce some of their works, however, and upon whom the future of Spanish drama rests, are Carlos Muñiz (1927) and Lauro Olmo (1923). Within Muñiz's theatre is found a little masterpiece, *El tintero* (*The Inkwell*, 1960), an expressionistic farce portraying the pressures of conformity in modern collective society. Lauro Olmo's first work, *La camisa* (*The Shirt*, 1962), already shows an "esperpentic" vision of reality, a hallmark of the modern realist dramatists. This particular work considers the oppression of poverty, hunger, and misery, particularly within the context of the Spanish emigration to Germany.

At its best, the theatre of twentieth-century Spain reflects an audacious and successful endeavour of self-renovation and regeneration. Prior to 1936, Salinas observed that there were two possible ways to relate to the public: flatter its taste or awaken new ideas. Max Aub took into consideration the fact that the public has to pay ticket prices generally beyond the means of the proletariat, and therefore to survive in the business of theatre authors conform to prevalent tastes. Dramatists who reacted against insipid theatre were not always successful, and often had their works produced in university theatres.[21]

The effort to write and produce a social theatre after 1936 was severely restricted by heavy censorship. Those who wrote in exile wrote for themselves or for other exiles, knowing full well their works would not be published in Spain. Now that the new regime has come about in Spain it is reasonable to expect that the plays of Alberti, Salinas, and Aub will be performed. Indeed, there will come a time in

---

María Rodríguez Méndez, José Martín Recuerda, Antonio Gala, José Ruibal, José María Bellido, Juan Antonio Castro, Jerónimo López Mozo, Manuel Martínez Mediero, and Luis Matilla, to name only a few who form the vanguard of the new movement in contemporary Spanish theatre. For an introduction to these dramatists see the already quoted works of George E. Wellwarth and Francisco Ruiz Ramón.

21 Barbara J. Heming, "The Spanish Theatre in Exile: 1939-1969" (Ph.D. dissertation, State University of N.Y. at Stony Brook, 1975), 7.

future decades when the works of the dramatists presented
in this essay will be regarded as a venerable, artistic embodi-
ment of an age, just as those of Lope de Vega and Calderón.

The theatre of twentieth-century Spain has been created
out of the search for humanistic values, particularly individual freedom. Paradoxical as it may seem, Spain's traditional
values are very twentieth century. In this vein Salvador de
Madariaga has observed that, "Spain's great freedom of
imagination is evident in her art, her universal literary figures, and in the discovery and colonizing of the New World;
man is the only subject of Spanish art and literature."[22]

---

22   Salvador de Madariaga, *Genius of Spain* (London: Oxford University
     Press, 1924), 42.

FIVE

IDEOLOGY AND STAGECRAFT IN THE HISPANIC-AMERICAN THEATRE OF THE 1960s

Kurt L. Levy
University of Toronto

T**hat** the Hispanic-American narrative enjoyed a period of unparalleled brilliance during the sixties can hardly be denied.[1] What is less frequently mentioned and probably less widely known is the fact that the so-called "boom" in prose fiction coincided with significant

---

1 "La prosa de ficción hispanoamericana—excluyendo unas obras, incluyendo otras según los gustos—tuvo un extraordinario período de auge en la década recién pasada" (José Donoso, *Historia personal del "boom"* [Barcelona, 1972], 11).

77

events on the Hispanic-American stage, though on a less
spectacular scale.[2] This paper seeks to address some of these
events in an attempt to define their social and human impact
as well as to examine the artistic devices which the dramatic
genre employed to capture Hispanic-American reality. I
have selected six representative plays from different geographic ambients, reflecting a variety in ideological and
human persuasion: one is from Puerto Rico, one from Central America, and the remaining four from the South American continent, two from the Northern sector, two from the
South. All of them share an abiding concern with twentieth-
century man in his human and social condition. "La
preocupación mía es el hombre y sus interrogantes o condición," Daniel Gallegos states in an interview;[3] most of his
playwright colleagues of the sixties would wholeheartedly
endorse this sentiment.[4]

It has been suggested, on the basis of internal evidence,
that the Chilean dramatist Egon Wolff (1926) had the
Chinese and Cuban revolutions in mind[5] when writing *Los*

2   "The decade of the nineteen sixties witnessed an unprecedented
    flourishing in the theatre arts of Latin America" (George W.
    Woodyard and Leon F. Lyday, "Studies on the Latin American
    Theatre, 1960-1969," *Theatre Documentation*, 2 [1969-70], 49).

3   From an interview reproduced in A. Herzfeld and T. Cajiao Salas
    (eds.), *El teatro de hoy en Costa Rica: Perspectiva crítica y antología* (San
    José, 1973), 123.

4   My textual references, inserted parenthetically, are to the following
    editions: Demetrio Aguilera Malta, *Infierno negro*, in Carlos Solór-
    zano (ed.), *El teatro actual latinoamericano (antología)* (México, 1972),
    291-338; Enrique Buenaventura, *En la diestra de Dios Padre*, in Carlos
    Solórzano (ed.), *El teatro hispanoamericano contemporáneo (antología)*,
    Vol. 1 (México, 1964), 262-307; Daniel Gallegos, *La colina*, in Anita
    Herzfeld and Teresa Cajiao Salas (eds.), *El teatro de hoy en Costa Rica
    (Perspectiva crítica y antología)* (San José, 1973), 132-92; Carlos Goros-
    tiza, *El pan de la locura*, in a volume (Buenos Aires, 1966) containing
    El puente, El pan de la locura (121-221), and *Los prójimos*; René Mar-
    qués, *El apartamiento*, in *Teatro*, Vol. 3 (Rio Piedras, 1971), 107-207;
    and Egon Wolff, *Los invasores*, in Carlos Solórzano (ed.), *El teatro
    hispanoamericano contemporáneo (antología)*, Vol. 1 (México, 1964),
    126-90.

5   See Orlando Gómez-Gil, *Historia crítica de la literatura his-
    panoamericana* (New York, 1968), 732; Leon F. Lyday, "Egon Wolff's
    Los invasores: A Play Within a Dream," *Latin American Theatre Review*
    (Fall, 1972), 19.

invasores (1962).[6] There is little doubt that the play reflects a vigorous ideological commitment and that it is intended to arouse the conscience of a middle class all too long oblivious to the concerns of the underdogs. Shocking the bourgeois out of his complacency is an obvious method of discharging the writer's responsibility.

Los invasores illustrates *par excellence* Wolff's ideological credo as well as his dramatic technique. There is a mood of vague anguish underlying the atmosphere of comfortable wealth in the home of industrialist Lucas Meyer. Our first glimpse of Lucas and Pietá is on the couple's return from a sumptuous ball. Their initial dialogue reveals instinctive fear that their seemingly secure bourgeois world may be in jeopardy. Pietá's premonition that the shadowy inhabitants of the shanty towns across the river are about to invade their sphere of influence is vaguely and paradoxically linked to her husband's consistent economic and social success: "Cuando todo sale bien me asusto" (p. 127). Lucas, who has been described as "invulnerable," shows that appearances are not borne out by reality, though he seeks to bolster his morale by remembering Schopenhauer's credo of the world being governed by self interest. "Nadie puede perturbar el orden establecido, porque todos están interesados en mantenerlo" (p. 132) seems to calm his fears temporarily.[7]

The conflict between the rich and the poor that was implicit in the introductory dialogue soon comes out into the open with the appearance of China, leader of the ragged figures from across the river, who stands for non-violent social change. In the ensuing debate between the industrialist and the beggar, the first of many, which basically are debates between Meyer and his own conscience, the invulnerability of Lucas is called into question. The wealthy indus-

---

6 This date, and the subsequent ones, are drawn from the bibliographies by Grismer, Hebblethwaite, and Neglia-Ordaz.

7 Leon Lyday identifies "guilt and fear" as principal themes of the play (see Lyday, "Egan Wolff's *Los invasores,*" 20), while Margaret S. Peden singles out fear as "possibly . . . the key word in a study of Wolff's theatre" (see Margaret S. Peden, "The Theater of Egon Wolff," in Leon F. Lyday and George W. Woodyard [eds.], *Dramatists in Revolt: The New Latin American Theater* [Austin, 1976], 197).

trialist shows himself to be a person of decidedly limited
scruples and social sense, willing, indeed eager, to get involved in traditional charities, and at the same time extremely reluctant to sacrifice the luxuries of his own life style.
In short, Lucas Meyer is the typical exponent of a social and
economic class, ever ready to rationalize and justify his own
position, and conscious of the function of words in human
and social relations.

The fundamental issue for the Chilean author, clearly a
dramatist concerned with ideas, is an enquiry into the essential nature of constructive and destructive forces. In other
words, who builds and who tends to tear down? China
charges the rich with exploitation and abuse, while Lucas
defends the capitalist position against the proletariat, insist-
ing (pp. 177-78) that he, Lucas Meyer, has generated happiness. There is a decided smug complacency in his proud
claim: "Esa es mi creación: hacer vidas" (p. 178). The proletariat has contributed little to life's happiness, Meyer
maintains, while the other side of his conscience intimates,
through China's response, that words have a strange habit of
confusing the issue: "Las palabras son inútiles" (p. 179). Con-
fronted with the charge that he is not adverse to amassing the
world's earthly goods, Meyer acknowledges the irrefutable
truth that "La codicia es el motor que mueve el mundo."
Little by little, the debates with China which scour Meyer's
conscience and lay bare unflattering motivations with ever-
increasing intensity lead the industrialist to the uncomforta-
ble realization that, notwithstanding his apparent invulnerability ("Firme como un roble, así es como voy a resistirte,"
p. 177), his shining social and human armour had developed
decided cracks. China's laconic summing up, "Hay mucha
tristeza en el mundo, Señor Meyer . . . pero hoy día, la es-
tamos venciendo," shows the author's ideological bias and his
formula for radical change.

The "generation gap" puts an added strain on an already
tense situation. Neither Marcela nor Bobby communicate
effectively with the invading hordes. Marcela's use of the
whip proves as counterproductive as does her brother's
grandiloquence. Such words as liberty, equality, and frater-

nity, when mouthed mechanically by a university student, take on a hollow ring and easily turn into senseless barking, devoid of meaning to the listeners and ultimately frustrating to the speaker. Yet there is one basic difference between Marcela and Bobby. Bobby is prepared to "olvidar y aprender," whereas Marcela is not able to adapt to the new regime. When Wolff has made his ideological point and China's dispassionate probing has wrested reluctant confessions from Meyer, the oneiric device seems to resolve the family's dilemma, but the collective sigh of relief is cut short by the appearance of the invading hand as the curtain falls, ominous sign that the living nightmare is about to begin for the Meyer family.[8]

Wolff's *Los invasores* has a special magic, blending a didactic message with poetic devices and enquiring into the complexity of truth and human identity.[9]

Two years separate *Los invasores* from *El apartamiento* (1964) by the Puerto Rican dramatist René Marqués (1919).[10] If *Los invasores* concerns social conflict as well as questions of human identity and truth, *El apartamiento* focusses on the anguish of modern man within a labyrinth of solitude. Marqués's human beings are trapped in an automated, sterilized microcosm, an absurd, dehumanized reality that precludes

---

8 How much of the play does the dream sequence encompass? Only the events subsequent to the introductory scene, after the Meyer family retires for the night, or the entire play? While most critics have tended towards the former view, Professor Lyday argues persuasively in favour of the latter (see Lyday, "Egon Wolff's *Los invasores*," 23ff.).

9 Frank Dauster observes that the playwright's apparent realism serves "para subrayar el elemento irreal" (Frank N. Dauster, *Historia del teatro hispanoamericano* [México, 1966], 91), and Willis Knapp Jones records a small but intriguing mechanical detail when he tells us that Wolff "plans his plays in English before writing them" (*Behind Spanish American Footlights* [Austin, 1966], 293). This brings to mind the "Teutonic logic and sense of order" that Peden discerns in Wolff's work.

10 Eleanor J. Martin's fine book-length study *René Marqués* (Boston, 1979) (Twayne's World Authors Series, 516) provides a detailed analysis of the author's writings. As far as *El apartamiento* is concerned, she points out that the play, "despite the rhetoric of the Indian figure, returns to the vivid portrayal of social ills in dramatic imagery" (p. 120).

all living dialogue. The play enquires into the dilemma of
Carola and Elpidio, fifty-eight and sixty years of age respectively, who are doomed to lead their purposeless lives in
complete isolation, in accordance with the melancholy message that spells out their dilemma and that is heard before
the curtain rises:

> Y les separaron del universo
> Y les robaron su humanidad
> Y les condenaron a vivir en el
> Más total apartamiento (p. 113).

Carola used to be an inspired poetess, Elpidio a brilliant
composer and pianist. Both have lost sight of their *raison
d'être*: communication has been replaced by the dehumanized milieu of their windowless apartment.[11] The
"hallucinating functionality" and efficient symmetry of their
abode smothers all living impulse and spontaneity, allowing
only insipid dialogue and the pursuit of such thoroughly
useless tasks as measuring unending quantities of blue ribbon or tackling an infinite puzzle. *El apartamiento* examines a
common challenge in its conflict between genius and frustration and in the inability of the two protagonists to face life
and reality. It is a depressingly human play which lacks the
caricaturesque effects and the poignant political intent of *Los
invasores*. Its message is universal and devoid of regional
flavour. (It is worth noting that the setting of *Los invasores* was
"un living de alta burguería. Cualquiera," whereas that of *El
apartamiento* is "un rincón cualquiera de las Américas.") The
proud indigenous figure, Tlo, is a blend of various native
tribes. Not unlike Terra and Lucío, the symbols of youth and
memory, Tlo introduces a moral problem when he pleads
with Carola and Elpidio to honour the promise offered once
upon a time by their creative genius.

   If Wolff's play deals basically with the inner conflict of one
person, since the dream sequence expresses Meyer's hopes

---

11 Elpidio and Carola "are reminiscent of Beckettian clowns playing
    their 'last game' in a claustrophobic interior" (Tamara Holzapfel,
    "The Theater of René Marqués: In Search of Identity and Form," in
    Lyday and Woodyard [eds.], *Dramatists in Revolt*, 160).

and fears, his illusions and frustrations ("tienes miedo, Lucas"), René Marqués's play examines the dilemma of two individuals, Carola and Elpidio, whose isolation is of their own choice and who fail ultimately because they refuse to recognize life's true purpose.[12] Therefore the central message of the play, recited before the curtain rises, might read more appropriately as follows:

> Se separaron del universo
> Se robaron su humanidad
> Se condenaron a vivir en el
> Más total apartamiento.

For Carola and Elpidio, there is no escape: there are no outside doors, no windows; no memories are permitted in the apartment. The word "antes" is frowned upon. The play opens with the exasperating routine of puzzle and blue ribbon; it ends after a total defeat of the momentary stimuli of Terra, Lucío, and Tlo, with the same exasperating, life-destroying monotony of routine, while the two protagonists await death as a liberating force.[13]

The question that the playwright raises by means of a seemingly absurd situation is far from absurd:What is our purpose in living? Puzzles and interminable blue ribbon? Marqués warns us that there are all too many people in this world whose special gifts cut them out for a "sacred mission" and who nonetheless prefer to evade their responsibility. Elpidio and Carola are afraid to "lose their apartment" and have to face reality and their own selves. Lucas Meyer subconsciously entertains an identical fear, as Pietá diagnoses, "Tienes miedo, Lucas."

The dilemma of Elpidio and Carola thus is universal. The character of Tlo who personifies the conscience of America

---

12   The personal solitude of the two protagonists "se refleja en la soledad física que les rodea" (Frank N. Dauster, "René Marqués y el tiempo culpable," in *Ensayos sobre teatro hispanoamericano* [México, 1975], 125).

13   Professor Holzapfels' interpretation, "Although the play conveys an almost overwhelming sense of anguish through isolation, its overall mood is not one of negation and futility" ("The Theater of René Marqués," in Lyday and Woodyard [eds.], *Dramatists in Revolt*, 161), differs from my own.

and the vitality of tradition—*lo nuestro*—constitutes an organic element of the play because he symbolizes the playwright's belief that America must be saved by means of the autochthonous element, the native essence. Elpidio and Carola reject the challenge of giving voice to the American conscience; failing in their sacred mission, they fail as individuals and as social beings.

El apartamiento accentuates its dramatic mood by dint of a number of visual and acoustic effects. Changes in lighting and sound accompany the different phases in the action. The struggle between civilization and barbarism singles out the sterile aspects of civilization and the fertile elements inherent in barbarism. The conflict between progress and tradition is expressed in terms of the struggle "entre música atonal y estridente moderna" (preparing the appearance of Landrilo and Cuprila) and "música dulce de flauta y caramillo de la región de los Andes" (introducing the appearance of Tlo). Marqués's social message is unmistakeable; so is his human credo.[14]

Wolff and Marqués scrutinize the individual mind and soul; the Argentine Carlos Gorostiza (1920) focusses on the collective phenomenon, the group in its everyday dealings. *El pan de la locura* (1958)[15] has been described as "la más completa de sus obras."[16] The beginning of the play takes us into a depressing milieu. It is the working area of a bakery on the outskirts of Buenos Aires whose general physical neglect defies the most elementary rules of hygiene. Even the all-pervading flour fails to camouflage effectively "la antigua y persistente suciedad del ambiente" (p. 123). We are soon made to realize that the human relations among the employees are an apt match for the sordid setting. The tango

---

14 Willis Knapp Jones terms Marqués "a nationalist in both art and politics" (*Behind Latin American Footlights*, 373). The playwright himself expresses unequivocal commitment when he states that "ser escritor es emprender una agónica e inacabable búsqueda de la verdad" (René Marqués, "La función del escritor puertorriqueño en el momento actual," *Ensayos* [Barcelona, 1972], 221).

15 I have used my author's prerogative to "extend" the sixties by two years so as to include Gorostiza's thought-provoking play.

16 See Carlos Solórzano, *El teatro actual latinoamericano* (México, 1972), 9.

that is heard as the curtain rises is grievously distorted and the dialogue is in tune with the physical decay. There are no bonds of friendship, no solidarity among the staff: each individual works for himself and defends his or her personal interests, though on occasions self-interest forges a temporary and usually rather frail alliance. The general overall impression is one of existentialist frustration, reflecting the dilemma of a group of people who hide their identity under masks or nicknames and who ignore the voice of their conscience, oblivious to their moral responsibility. Not unlike Lucas, Pietá, Elpidio, and Carola, they are instinctively afraid of truth, because truth brings with it moral responsibility. Appearances challenge realities at every step: Antonio, the foreman, is a good example. According to Juana, Antonio is a happy individual: "se ríe, nada más" (p. 137). Nothing could be further from the truth. Antonio is basically a victim of a frustration going back to a childhood episode. The traumatic words "El drama había fallado" (p. 139) linger on to remind him of his humiliation and turn into a *leitmotiv* for his personality. Antonio hides under a smiling exterior, the Polish-Jew Abraham has become José, and Lupo is known as Badoglio, which dictates his exasperatingly photographic veteran's memory for the military details of the Second World War.

The everyday, humdrum activities are suddenly interrupted by the arrival of the new assistant, Mateo, who injects a positive human flavour into the depressing milieu. He is an ingenuous individual who is introduced as a timid youth of few words but whose torrential response to questions soon disenchants his listeners as to his true personality. Mateo serves as catalyst: his persistent seemingly innocent questions come to grips with reality and true identity, challenging mask and hypocrisy. Within this context of appearances and self-deception where people do not know themselves and are afraid of the truth of their own identities, Mateo seems to play the rôle of the child who discovers that "the Emperor has no clothes," discerning the moral nudity of his companions. It is Mateo who tells the authentic episode of the "bread of insanity" that occurred in France.

Mateo's appearance brings hidden tensions into the open and triggers moral problems, under the disguise of innocent questions concerning the flour which becomes identified with the mysterious epileptic attacks that have haunted the district and with the French episode told by Mateo. The moral dilemma turns into a painful conflict between loyalty to the employer and his bakery and the individual conscience. When Mateo questions the purity of the flour ("está fea," p. 156), he gives voice to everyone's instinctive preoccupation. The question of moral responsibility is the logical next step, and with it the question of moral guilt in terms of individual or collective responsibility. Everyone realizes that the survival of the twelve-year-old business is at stake—a dilemma which brings to mind Ibsen's *The Enemy of the People*. Whose duty is it to speak up and make the official accusation, the employer's or the employee's? Antonio takes refuge behind the memories of his childhood humiliation ("la comedia había fallado") as he rejects his moral responsibility. Badoglio on the other hand rationalizes himself into a comfortable justification of his failure to respond to the moral challenge inherent in the situation, and he does so by dint of the most insidious of all arguments. Badoglio, like all too many other Badoglios, confesses: "No quiero ningún lío; ya tuve bastantes" (p. 179). No one wants problems; everyone is afraid. Once again, central concerns of *Los invasores* and *El apartamiento* come vividly to mind. The accusation does materialize in the end: it does not come from any of the employees, but from the employer's wife Juana ("Sí, llamé yo," p. 188), whose motivations evidently do not lie in the field of public hygiene.

The nagging question becomes increasingly persistent: Who bears the moral blame, the individual giving the orders, or the group who submits to them and carries them out? The owner's position is as easily understandable as is that of Lucas Meyer in his debates with the leader of the invading hordes. He uses sentimentality as well as verbal violence to defend his livelihood against his employees, who at this moment present a united front. Curiously enough, the flour problem and the intervention of young Mateo ("con ingenua y simpática

suficiencia," p. 191) have succeeded in forging a social conscience in these constitutionally frustrated and frightened
individuals. The decisive change in their moral and social
attitude is brought out most clearly at the critical moment
when the owner decides to fire Mateo whom he regards as
the principal trouble maker. Garufa's quiet but determined
protest on behalf of the group, "Usted no puede hacer eso,
patrón" (p. 201), reveals a unique show of solidarity and
signals a totally new phase in the employer-employee relationship. It is truly an interesting psychological touch that the
person who triggers this new relationship is the very man
whose first appearance in the bakery had prompted an instinctive antagonism on the part of his new colleagues. "Me
pone nervioso" (p. 155), acknowledges Antonio when asked
to define his impression of the new colleague. At the end the
collective protest takes place under Mateo's banner: Fuente
Ovejuna repudiates the yoke of tyranny.

Yet the collective response which ushers in a new era in
employer-staff relations does not provide the key to the
human and moral dilemmas. Juana's impassioned speech
(p. 211) not only defines the frustration of her own existence,
but goes a long way towards summing up the dilemma of the
others who through fear of "líos" have failed to shoulder
their share of moral responsibility. The issue is squarely between Mateo's unassuming, life-giving philosophy "Ha-
ciendo cosas pequeñas se llega igual" (p. 192) and Juana's
outburst of existentialist hopelessness:

Muéstrele bien todo eso; que sepa cómo amasamos ese pan; cómo
comemos ese pan. Cuéntele cómo pasamos cada día dando vueltas
y vueltas, agarrados a esta rueda idiota que no lleva a ninguna
parte, hundiéndonos cada vez más . . . ensuciándonos cada vez
más . . . amasando, comiendo, amasando y volviendo a comer esa
cosa sucia y miserable. Y explíquele por qué nadie tiene valor para
soltarse. Ni usted, ni yo, ni Lupo . . . ni mi marido. Nadie. Dígale al
muchacho. Háblele del miedo. Que sepa que nuestra culpa está ahí.
Que el veneno sigue ahí, digan lo que digan esos hombres! (p. 211).

Having been taken to task by the two inspectors whom her
own accusation had summoned to the bakery, she receives
her climactic rebuke from Antonio, who rejects her and

decides to leave with Mateo. His words "No, patrona . . . sería como volver a hacer ese pan, con esa misma harina" (p. 127) spell the doom of her hopes and at the same time make it clear that Mateo's presence had not only brought about a radical change in the behaviour of the social group but had also effected a maturing process in individuals. Antonio recognizes as a result the elusive shades of freedom which are more apparent than real: Juana's brand of freedom is not his own, and he must reject her.

El pan de la locura comes to grips with universal problems[17] in a regional attire, replete with regional idiom. It shows on an existentialist plane how appearances confront reality, responsibility is curbed by cowardice, freedom of choice is challenged at the individual and collective levels, and how Man's desperate struggle to give voice to his true identity often runs aground on the rocky shoals of fear.[18]

La colina by the Costa Rican dramatist Daniel Gallegos (1930) was first performed in 1960 and published the year after.[19] The mainspring of the action is the meaning of God, and the manner in which the polemical theme[20] is introduced smacks of the theatre of the absurd. Gregorio, a habitual drunk, and his wife, Mercedes, a hard-working woman whose patience with her hard-drinking husband has worn thin, live with their imbecilic son Manuelito in a hut in the mountains where they offer food and lodging to the pilgrims visiting a near-by sanctuary. The absurd element is injected

17   Isaac Chocrón observes that Gorostiza tends to present "dentro de un realismo severo, ideas filosóficas y casi metafísicas" ("Palabras preliminares" to Gorostiza, *Juana y Pedro* [Caracas, 1976]).

18   "This play is an excellent and straightforward examination of individual conscience in a real-life setting" (Merlin H. Forster,"The Theater of Carlos Gorostiza," in Lyday and Woodyard [eds.], *Dramatists in Revolt*, 116).

19   "*La colina* es una obra bien estructurada alrededor de un contenido temático profundo, de gran actualidad. Callegos . . . lleva su obra a un plano de universalidad" (Anita Herzfeld and Teresa Cajiao Salas, *El teatro de hoy en Costa Rica: Perspectiva crítica y antología* [San José, 1973], 127).

20   "El anuncio del estreno de *La colina* provocó gran controversia en el público constarricense y se entabló una agitada polémica por la prensa" (ibid., 126).

with the news transmitted by radio that the United Nations have proclaimed the death of God and the preparations for his official funeral are in progress. This explosive piece of news provides the catalyst for what the author describes as an "auto sacramental" in which clerics and lay people interact and each character responds to the transcendental event in his or her individual manner. What started out as a grandiose "liberation game," based on absolute candour and presumably freedom from God's restraining and inhibiting influence, soon turns into a grandiose dilemma because, though God has been eliminated by official human decree, the internal God, our conscience, remains very much alive, and the relativity of freedom is laid bare. The theoretical liberation proves a dismal farce, though with many spicy revelations and one redeeming feature: the news of the United Nations decree removes the mask of deceit and hypocrisy and leads to a disclosure—albeit a reluctant one at times—of each character's true motivation and, not unlike the result of Mateo's role in *El pan de la locura*, to a questioning of his or her identity.

At the end of the play, with all-too-evident symbolism, the fog that covered the mountain at the beginning has cleared. "Hace un lindo día" (p. 191), since each one of the protagonists has been able to clarify his or her role in life. Those without genuine faith acknowledge this fact by descending from the mountain, whereas the others remain. Each of the characters identifies his or her peculiar brand of "freedom," his or her "reality," and acts accordingly. The Mother Superior and Father José abandon the mountain, while Gregorio and Mercedes, in a complete about-face, decide to keep the inn open for those in need and to endeavour to make their shaky marriage last and care for Manuelito with greater affection than before. Tomás the sceptic, who in the introductory scene had denied the existence of God ("Para mí no ha muerto . . . porque nunca ha existido," p. 137), undergoes an astounding conversion, discovering God through his love for Marta, and the latter, no doubt the key character in the play, notes that she has been "restored" to God, precisely through the intercession of "doubting Thomas." "Nunca estuve tan llena de Dios como ahora," she acknowledges in an obvious reference to a process of mutual salvation.

Joselino's words in the closing scene, "Ya no hay niebla" (p. 191), sum up the salutary effects of the extraordinary night. Different from the totally negative dénouement of *El apartamiento*, Gallegos's message is positive, since each one of his characters discovers his or her true identity and a potentially constructive role in life. It is not hard to recognize the playwright's genuine commitment to his fellowmen and his deep conviction that God is very much alive and that our love and compassion are tangible expressions of his presence.[21]

The evident echoes of the theatre of the absurd tend to underline the validity of the ideological issues which the playwright broaches in *La colina*. The strict adherence of the unities and the consistency in theme and character presentation intensify the dramatic impact of a powerful play, notwithstanding its overly facile symbolism.[22]

Infierno negro by the Ecuadorean Demetrio Aguilera Malta (1909) appeared in 1967, coinciding with the publication of "il mondo fantastico e violento de *Cien años de soledad*."[23] Aguilera Malta's play is a hard-hitting expressionistic approach to the problem of black emancipation, showing the same unmistakeable commitment that the author displays in his prose fiction.[24] Expressionism conjures up a magic world of its own.[25] The expressionist does not copy reality; he seeks

---

21   The author makes his literary purpose clear in an interview: "La preocupación mía es el hombre y sus interrogantes o condición. . . . El único compromiso en el que yo creo es el compromiso con mi conciencia" (ibid., 123).

22   Willis Knapp Jones lamented in 1966 that "Costa Rica is still far from achieving her national drama" (Jones, *Latin American Footlights*, 425). Daniel Gallegos would appear to be a promising name towards attainment of that goal.

23   Giuseppe Bellini, *Il Labirinto magico* (Milano, 1973).

24   Ricardo Descalzi notes: "Representa una protesta, con patéticas descripciones del martrio del negro en su vida cotidiana, entre el medio blanco" (Pedro F. de Andrea, *Demetrio Aguilera Malta: Bibliografía* [México, 1969], 10).

25   This movement of ideological reform, with its antecedents in Germany, repudiated the prevailing social order as hollow and dehumanized. Making their revolutionary point with more or less polemical fervour, the young expressionists advocated the utopian

to explore what he considers its authentic core, ultimate reality as it were. Setting, characters, and stage technique reflect this distinctive approach to the theatre—an approach in which peculiar traits are made to stand out, and in which the emphasis is on suggestion rather than portrayal, and caricaturesque distortion is utilized to drive home an ideological message.

The play's geography is divided broadly between life and death, Nilónpolis and Necrópolis, although the former which ostensibly represents life reflects moral decay with its poisonous prejudices and petty irrational hatreds. Necrópolis on the other hand, ostensibly symbolizing death, includes a living dimension, erasing the idea of total death and proclaiming by means of the chorus that "Nadie muere del todo, ni se acaba" (p. 320). The climactic concept is a tribute to life: "Vivo, estoy vivo, y salgo de la muerte" (p. 321). It is an optimistic, life-giving message for those who triumph ultimately; for those who are condemned, however, the answer is eternal punishment—*infierno negro*.

The human substance is provided by blacks and whites, types who identify themselves by means of characteristic traits or gestures. The majority of the black characters are nameless and bear numbers (Negro 1, 2, 3, 4): their rôle is

emergence of a "new man." For further details on expressionism, "movimiento de corta vigencia, pero de amplia trascendencia," and on Aguilera's theatre, see Gerardo Luzuriaga's informative thesis "Demetrio Aguilera Malta dramaturgo" (Ph.D. dissertation, University of Iowa, 1969) (*Comprehensive Dissertation Index 1861-1972* [Ann Arbor, Mich., 1973], 813), published in book form in 1973 as *Del realismo al expresionismo: el teatro de Aguilera Malta* (Madrid, 1973). It contains a fifty-page, detailed analysis of *Infierno negro* and reaches the conclusion that the play "marca el punto culminante en el desarrollo del teatro aguileriano desde el realismo hasta el expresionismo" (p. 182). Another doctoral thesis on Aguilera Malta which includes consideration of the playwright and specifically *Infierno negro* is Clementine Christos Rabassa's "Epic Elements in the Works of Demetrio Aguilera Malta" (Ph.D. dissertation, Columbia University, 1971) (*Comprehensive Dissertation Index 1861-1972* [Ann Arbor, Mich., 1973], 669). Dr. Rabassa's fine thesis (which detects a "pervasive epic spirit" in Aguilera Malta's literary panorama) appeared in book form last year as *Demetrio Aguilera Malta and Social Justice* (London, 1980).

one of giving voice in poetic form to ideological truths.
Aguilera Malta selected prominent examples of *poesía negra*
and incorporated them into his play: the magic effect of this
device allays some of the deliberate incongruities of the rest
of the play. ("Cada vez que los negros recitan, la representa-
ción debe asumir un nivel mágico," p. 295.)[26]

The whites on the other hand have scant magic. They are
described as animals, endowed with adjectives which are
designed to underline their negative human substance.
There is Mater Salamandra, laden down with jewels; there is
Arácnido Mefítico; there is Creso Topo, the renowned
banker with the mechanical and stereotyped smile; there is
Feto Eunuco, who is in charge of public relations and is the
last word in fashion; there is Alondra Escuálida, who is rarely
sober; and of course there is the illustrious soldier Pimpam-
pum whose comments are rather elementary and lacking in
variety: "Grrr-Grrr." They are stereotypes, symbolic of su-
perficiality, materialism, and prejudice. The blacks are the
victims and the whites the vultures who exploit without
compassion.

The author's intense ideological concern is conveyed by
means of a number of devices, such as colours (the blacks'
distinctive tunics come to mind), lighting effects ("el reflector
focaliza"), and music, as well as by dint of characteristic
gestures. Aguilera Malta uses the dramatic genre for the
same purpose as the novel and the short story, i.e., to defend
the underdogs, in this case "negro que fuiste para el algodón
de U.S.A., para la caña dulce del Brasil" (p. 295). Going
further, and reminiscent of the "new man" concept of early
expressionism, he advocates tolerance in a somewhat utopian state where no race has "el monopolio de la belleza, de la
inteligencia y de la fuerza" (p. 338).

The language of the play offers a stimulating blend of
prose and verse, the former accompanying the sordid
exploits of the notables of the city of Nilónpolis, the latter
providing the "magic level" for the appearances of the

---

26 The playwright had this to say in an interview: "El clima poético se
presta para la comunión mágica" (Luzuriaga, *Del realismo al expresionismo*, 201).

blacks.[27] This element, drawn from the verse of distinguished exponents of *poesía negra*, underlines ancestral tradition, the roots, "lo nuestro," exalted by René Marqués in *El apartamiento*. The play, which begins by lamenting the melancholy fate of the "negro huidor, negro cautivo, negro rebelde" and upbraids the white race for its narrowmindedness and lack of sensitivity, ends on a reaffirmation of the author's impassioned commitment and on an optimistic note: "Para todos hay lugar en la cita de la victoria." Notwithstanding the dismal record of centuries, Aguilera Malta glimpses a ray of hope, *victoria* being the closing word as the curtain goes down.[28]

When W. O. Galbraith observes that "Colombia is surprisingly poor in dramatic works,"[29] he no doubt echoes a view that is widely held. Colombia is a land of poets (and some renowned novelists), but not dramatists. Yet it is fair to say that playwrights of note are beginning to emerge on the Colombian scene.

Antonio Alvarez Lleras (1892-1956)[30] and Luis Enrique Osorio (1896-1966), both strongly committed to social reform, may be the most significant names of the first half of this century; Enrique Buenaventura (1925), hailing from Cali, stands out on the contemporary dramatic scene. His delightful play *En la diestra de Dios Padre* took first prize at the

---

27　Aguilera Malta's stylistic formula in *Infierno negro* fits the title of Giuseppe Bellini's anthology *Realismo magico en denuncia nel romanzo di Demetrio Aguilera Malta*; it fuses organically magic realism and protest.

28　Defining the function of literature, Aguilera Malta explains: "Soy un hombre libre a quien le interesan mucho los problemas de los otros hombres. A plantearlos y solucionarlos quiero contribuir con mis expresiones estéticas... no creo en lo estético 'puro;' la literatura para mí es una expresión de la vida" (Luzuriaga, *Del realismo al expresionismo*, 200). (Carlos Fuentes, it may be recalled, rejected the "luxury" of pure literature as inimical to the Latin American cultural fabric.)

29　W. O. Galbraith, *Colombia: A General Survey* (London, 1966), 37.

30　Leon F. Lyday wrote his doctoral thesis at the University of North Carolina on "The Dramatic Art of Antonio Alvarez Lleras" (1966) (*Comprehensive Dissertation Index, 1861-1972* [Ann Arbor, Mich., 1973] 814 [27/08, p. 2534A]). (Often referred to as a social dramatist... "his best works nonetheless are his historical drama and his two psychological dramas.")

Paris Festival in 1960.[31] It is based on Tomás Carrasquilla's
finest short story by the same title, which in turn is a master-
ful reworking of one of the most ancient and most popular
themes in universal folklore, i.e., that of a supernatural vis-
itor who grants a number of wishes.[32] Buenaventura's play
(and of course Carrasquilla's *cuento*) are generously endowed
with local colour in setting, character, and language.[33]
The distinctive Department of Antioquia in Colombia's An-
dean region provides the geographic, human, and linguistic
raw material. While *Infierno negro* unfolded against a background divided between life and death, Buenaventura's play
moves among three locales: heaven, earth, and hell. The
human beings, however, who are involved in the action are
most assuredly of local vintage. They are individuals who
dress, eat, drink, and talk like *gentes de mi lugar* (p. 263).

It may be worth remembering that Carrasquilla termed his
cuento simply "un folklore que pinta nuestro pueblo."[34] It is
the story of a poor man, Peralta, who is granted five wishes in
recognition of his hospitality and charity. The universal
theme includes such "regional" characters as Jesus, Saint
Peter, the Devil, and Death herself, all of whom appear *en
disfraz paisa*, sport colourful *ruanas*, eat *arepas* and *quesito*,
and drink chocolate. Peralta is a kindly person who insists on
performing charitable deeds despite his own destitute condition, his motto being: "Mi familia son los prójimos" (p. 266).
His charity is misinterpreted time and again and the very
recipients of his generosity gossip behind his back and take
advantage of him. His elderly sister is particularly vocal in

---

31   For further details, see Oscar Collazos, "Trayectoria del teatro
     escuela de Cali," *Letras Nacionales* (Bogotá), 8 (May-June 1966),
     25-27.
32   For further details, see Kurt L. Levy, *Tomás Carrasquilla*, Twayne's
     World Authors Series, 546 (Boston, 1980), 54-57, as well as 134-35
     (note 14).
33   Erminio Neglia's informative *Aspectos del teatro moderno his-
     panoamericano* (Bogotá, 1975) contains a brief reference to
     Buenaventura's play in his essay "Temas y rumbos del teatro rural
     hispanoamericano del siglo xx" (p. 57).
34   Letter by Carrasquilla, dated Medellín, August 14, 1936 (Tomás
     Carrasquilla, *Obras completas*, Vol. 2 [Medellín, 1958], 808).

criticizing his *sangre de gusano* because it affects her self-interest. Others show similar concern. When Peralta's astuteness forces Death to "take a holiday," the grave-digger logically resents seeing his livelihood in jeopardy and gives his grievance a personal focus: "Y agora hay más ricos que antes y más pobres y todo sigue lo mismo. Sólo que no hay muertos y eso sí es una calamidá" (p. 285).

In as far as Buenaventura's "mojiganga ejemplar" displays Carrasquilla's basic ingredients, it involves *gentes de mi lugar* with a distinctively local behaviour pattern and local idiom. But the emphasis has shifted.[35] Whereas Carrasquilla was mainly concerned with telling a good story with a gentle moral twist, Buenaventura uses colourful regional folklore to satirize the folly of attempting to "rock the boat," even with the purest of intentions ("el mundo no puede cambiar y asina como está hecho se debe dejar," p. 303), and drive home the sobering truth that, in a world ruled overwhelmingly by self interest, "nada se paga tan caro . . . como ser bueno" (p. 281). The lively play, full of boisterous humour and human truth, offers a fitting illustration of its author's tenet that "el teatro popular . . . deberá caracterizarse por el uso de las fuentes populares tales como la mojiganga de Antioquia y el sainete costeño."[36] Buenaventura's creative curve leads from the folkloric theatre, a regional subject *contado y cantado*, with gradually increasing social flavour as we have seen, to the dramatist's impassioned conviction that the theatre must be instrumental in bringing about social change: "Tenemos que luchar por una verdadera politización del arte y por hacer conscientes de lo que es el arte y significa a las fuerzas que necesitan cambiar la sociedad."[37]

---

35 Gerardo Luzuriaga's interesting article, "*En la diestra de Dios Padre* y la contextualización histórica del folclore," in *Narradores Latinoamericanos 1929-1979* (Caracas, 1980), 127-43, examines four different versions of Buenaventura's play and studies its textual and ideological evolution, as well as its debt to, and growing departure from, Carrasquilla's *cuento*.

36 Maida Watson Espener, "La teoría teatral de Enrique Buenaventura," in Maida Watson Espener and Carlos José Reyes (eds.), *Materiales para una historia del teatro en Colombia* (Bogotá, 1978), 354.

37 Enrique Buenaventura, "Teatro y cultura," in ibid., 296.

The 1960s are a remarkable decade for Hispanic-American letters. Particularly prose fiction sharpens its focus, defining and interpreting American man, enquiring into his identity, and altogether spelling out the magic of America with a wealth of stylistic and structural detail. The Nobel Prize for Literature, for the first time in the history of the prestigious award, goes to a Latin-American novelist (Miguel Angel Asturias, 1967).

Yet drama too comes into its own, and life clearly is its essence. It is a theatre of living people, close to Latin America's social reality and its individual and collective hopes and fears. *Los invasores* probes the guilt of an individual within the social context at the conscious and subconscious levels, *El apartamiento* the guilt of two individuals who evade their responsibility as human beings and creative artists, their "sacred mission" as potential interpreters of their native cultural legacy ("lo nuestro"). *El pan de la locura* scrutinizes the question of collective guilt in a milieu of human and physical neglect whose inhabitants prefer to shirk their responsibilities ("evitar líos") until young Mateo strips them of their masks and forces them to confront their true identity and reality. "No cabe la menor duda de que, sea quien sea el futuro maestro de pala, Antonio y Mateo estarán presentes cada vez que se amase el pan en esta cuadra de panadería." There is an abiding social concern in all these plays, with fear as one of the chief motivating forces, coupled with such weighty issues as moral responsibility, the relativity of truth, and the perplexing conflict between appearance and reality. *La colina* adds a new dimension, i.e., the impact of religion on human affairs, the role and meaning of God becoming intertwined with such questions as freedom and the moral conscience. *Infierno negro* uses expressionist technique to formulate its powerful social message, and *En la diestra de Dios Padre* injects a refreshing humorous note into a literary panorama which, according to Uslar Pietri, tends to smile all too infrequently.[38]

---

38   Hispanic American literature "sonríe poco. El buen humor le es extraño" (Arturo Uslar Pietri, *Breve historia de la novela hispanoamericana* [Caracas, 1954], 167).

There is an intringuing relationship between *apartamiento* and *invasores* phenomena which almost assumes *leitmotiv* dimensions. In four of the plays discussed, a haunting *apartamiento* pattern prevails, physically and spiritually, with strict adherence to the unities, until an invading force challenges the validity of the pattern, triggering positive or negative responses. The weighty debate of God's impact on human affairs takes place in a locale which is just as hermetically sealed as is the dehumanized abode where two tired old people seek refuge from living challenges in interminable exercises of futility. *Apartamiento* rules in the sloppy Buenos Aires bakery where individual responsibility is on trial—as it does in the elegant *living* where a wealthy industrialist vainly seeks to silence the nagging voice of his conscience.

It stands to reason that the esthetic calibre of these plays is not measured in terms of their ideological message. Croce's point is well taken, though polemically extreme: ideological literature tends to sin on two counts, as ideology and as literature. Rodríguez Monegal calls attention to the continuing validity of a very old truth: the message of a work of literature is in its language. In other words the *qué* is secondary to the *cómo*,[39] which brings to mind Pope's attractive definition of originality: "True wit is nature to advantage dressed / What oft was thought but ne'er so well expressed."

As Leon Lyday states quite properly in his lucid analysis of *Los invasores*, "the play's the thing,"[40] and ideology is merely one facet of the artistic whole—albeit a significant one where a theatre of ideas is involved.

---

39 César Fernández Moreno, "Tradición y renovación," in *América Latina en su literatura* (México, 1972), 163.
40 Leon Lyday, "Egon Wolff's *Los invasores*," 19-20.